The Great Savings and Loan Debacle

James R. Barth

The AEI Press

Publisher for the American Enterprise Institute

WASHINGTON, D.C.

1991

James R. Barth, the former chief economist of the Federal Home Loan Bank Board and the Office of Thrift Supervision, September 1987 to November 1989, is the Lowder Eminent Scholar in Finance at Auburn University.

Distributed by arrangement with

University Press of America, Inc.
4720 Boston Way   3 Henrietta Street
Lanham, Md. 20706   London WC2E 8LU England

3 5 7 9 10 8 6 4 2

AEI Special Analyses 91-1

Printed in the United States of America

For Mary and Rachel Barth

Acknowledgments

Many individuals assisted me in the preparation of this book. Most important was Dan Brumbaugh, who not only first introduced me to the problems of the savings and loan industry but cowrote several papers that have heavily influenced my thinking about the problems. He has been a continual source of encouragement and motivation. Other coauthors who have provided valuable assistance are George Benston, Michael Bradley, Peter Elmer, John Feid, Carl Hudson, Bob Keleher, Carol Labich, Dan Page, Marty Regalia, Gabriel Riedel, Hamp Tunis, George Wang, David Whidbee, Philip Wiest, and, most of all, Philip Bartholomew. Other individuals who assisted me through their writings or discussions are Bob Auerbach, Bill Black, Jim Boland, Charles Calomiris, Andrew Carron, Roger Craine, Jacob Dreyer, Bert Ely, Catherine England, Bill Ferguson, Jim Follain, Gillian Garcia, Ed Golding, Gary Gorton, Stuart Greenbaum, Dan Gropper, Ben Gup, Jack Guttentag, Frank Haas, John Hand, Bill Haraf, Eric Hemel, Paul Horvitz, Tom Huertas, Milton Joseph, George Kaufman, Herb Kaufman, Roger Kormendi, Mike Laub, Pat Lawler, Bob Litan, G. S. Maddala, Mary Maginniss, Harry Meyers, Reid Nagle, Ray Natter, Richard Nelson, Lou Noyd, Jim Pearce, Perry Quick, Steve Redburn, Ken Scott, Gene Sherman, Don Simonson, Stacy Sirmans, Fred Smith, Lewis Spellman, P. A. V. B. Swamy, Melanie Tammen, Haluk Unal, Bob Van Order, John Weicher, Larry White, Mark Wohar, and especially Ed Kane, who has always willingly provided me with extremely helpful comments and suggestions ever since I first focused on the savings and loan industry.

I also wish to thank Rebecca Blanchard and Sherree Durham for their excellent assistance in the preparation of this book. In particular, without Sherree's persistence the book could not have been completed in a timely manner. Finally, a deep debt of gratitude is owed John Makin for asking me to write the book and then graciously granting me a two-month extension when my schedule became quite hectic.

Contents

List of Figures

1
Introduction

During the 1980s the savings and loan industry experienced its worst performance in its 160-year existence. Over the period 525 insolvent institutions were liquidated or sold at an estimated present-value cost to the federal insurer of savings and loans of $47 billion. Another eighteen institutions were simply stabilized, and hence still awaiting final disposition, at an estimated present-value cost of $7 billion. Despite all these closures, still another 517 institutions were reporting insolvency but were still operating at the end of the decade. It was estimated in the spring of 1990 that these remaining candidates for closure would cost $100 billion or more in present-value terms. Furthermore, at least a thousand more savings and loans began the decade of the 1990s seriously troubled and attempting to survive the massive consolidation, shrinkage, and restructuring that began sweeping through the industry in the late 1980s.

The most disturbing aspect of the great savings and loan debacle is that taxpayers have been required to bear the major portion of the cleanup cost for this private industry. This obligation follows directly from the way the federal deposit insurance system was structured when established during the Great Depression. Depositors who put their funds in insured accounts were told they would be fully protected against any and all losses. The intent of the federal government was to instill enough confidence in depositors that they would never again engage in widespread and disruptive runs on depository institutions as they did in the early 1930s. As a secondary goal, federal deposit insurance was to protect all small depositors. In addition to these two goals, taxpayers were to be protected from any losses incurred by depository institutions. This protection was to be provided through

1

an elaborate regulatory and supervisory structure whose aim was to contain the risk-taking behavior by insured depository institutions and to cover any costs of failure from a reserve fund established by premiums levied on the deposits at all insured institutions. Protecting taxpayers was an important goal, but one that the government has clearly failed to achieve. Indeed, the government took actions that not only made matters far worse than they otherwise would have been in the beleaguered savings and loan industry but also systematically underestimated the size of the problem throughout the 1980s.

It is crucial that the facts of this debacle be told. Only by understanding exactly what happened and why can we take the appropriate actions to prevent a similar situation from occurring. Many argue that the story is quite simple: some owners of savings and loans became greedy and engaged in excessively risky activities when the industry was deregulated in the early 1980s, while others simply looted their institutions. Although these things undeniably happened, they account for only a portion of the story—and a small portion at that. The savings and loan industry was in fact insolvent, and deeply so, even before deregulation occurred. And neither fraud nor insider abuse caused the insolvency. Deregulation and illegal activities only exacerbated an already grave situation. The reason for the plight of savings and loans at the beginning of the 1980s was a heavy concentration of assets in residential mortgage loans that had been booked at fixed rates years earlier but that were being funded with deposits paying the much higher market interest rates then current.

Interestingly, though, normal market forces are not responsible for the heavy investment of institutions in fixed-rate residential mortgage loans. Instead, the government greatly influenced the behavior of savings and loans not only by providing significant tax incentives to use most deposits to fund home purchases but also by prohibiting institutions from meaningfully diversifying their portfolios and even offering appropriate adjustable-rate loans until the early 1980s. The stage was therefore set for the disaster that struck the savings and loan industry in the 1980s. The industry was virtually a time bomb waiting to explode when interest rates skyrocketed in the late 1970s and early 1980s.

Without access to federally insured deposits, would savings and loans have ever experienced their sharp postwar growth while remaining heavily exposed to the risk associated with "lending

long and borrowing short"? With no incentive on the part of insured depositors to discipline the institutions, savings and loans
were given great leeway to tap a sizable and expanding pool of
savings over the years. When the interest rate bomb finally ex-
ploded and devastated the entire industry, the government's be-
lated response was to enact legislation granting savings and loans
new and expanded powers to engage in activities similar to those
of commercial banks. The rationale was apparently that if savings
and loans operated more like commercial banks, they would be
less exposed to interest rate risk. The broader powers, however,
came far too late to undo the damage already done.

Rather than openly disclose the size of the problem, in the
early 1980s the government took actions to make it less visible.
Capital requirements were reduced, lax regulatory accounting
standards were employed, the federal tax code was changed to
benefit acquirers of troubled institutions, and mergers were arranged that eliminated some of the insolvencies by creating an
asset called goodwill that immediately increased reported regulatory capital. This policy of capital forbearance was based on
the apparent hope that these greater powers would ease the difficulties until interest rates came down and then protect these
institutions from similar problems in the future. After all, from
the perspective of the government, the industry had encountered
interest rate problems in the mid-1960s and then again in the early
1970s and survived them. Why not gamble once again that the
industry's problem was related solely to interest rates and would
soon go away?

This time, unfortunately, the regulatory gamble ended in
disaster. There were, however, some signs for optimism in the
mid-1980s: interest rates did decline, and the majority of savings
and loans once again began reporting regulatory accounting profits. Yet, hundreds upon hundreds of institutions continued to report insolvency without being reorganized or closed by the government. Even more were reporting near insolvency. The *truly*
insolvent institutions certainly had every incentive to gamble for
resurrection. More generally, by offering higher rates on their
deposits than competitors, inadequately capitalized institutions
could obtain the funds with which to invest in high-risk activities.
This perfectly legal strategy was simply an institution's attempt
to grow out of its troubles with the assurance that any gains would
accrue to the owners and any losses would be borne by the federal

3

insurer. Only with access to federally insured funds and lax regulation and supervision could such a go-for-broke strategy be pursued. Excessive risk taking and even fraud flourished in an environment of virtually nonexistent market discipline and totally inadequate government constraints.

This is the story that must be told. All the blame for the great savings and loan debacle cannot be placed on fraud and deregulation. Instead, these factors only intensified the problems created by a flawed federal deposit insurance system and regulatory and supervisory structure. This book argues that the major blame for the debacle rests with the government—Congress, the administration, and the federal (and state) regulator and insurer of savings and loans—and therefore that the government alone has the responsibility for reforming the way in which discipline is imposed upon the nation's depository institutions. All the legislation enacted in the 1980s was simply a short-sighted response to an immediate problem and therefore failed to provide a longer-term solution to the underlying problems of the federally insured depository institutions. We need reform with a longer-term focus, that is, a system in which the private sector's quest for profits is kept in check by its aversion to losses, thus more adequately protecting taxpayers.

In the remainder of the book, chapter 2 chronicles the growth and development of savings and loans from their origin in 1831 to the modern crisis years beginning in 1980. The institutional design of the savings and loan is seen as a natural and successful response to market forces in the early years. Savings and loans specialized in financing home ownership with savings deposits, a service that the other financial institutions then in existence were not providing. Commercial banks, in particular, specialized in financing business activities with demand deposits. As market forces gradually changed over time, however, the institutional design of the savings and loan became increasingly inflexible as a result of the growing involvement of first the state and then the federal government in the regulation and supervision of the industry. The inability to evolve in response to changing market forces set the stage for the present troubles.

Chapter 3 describes the crisis years of the 1980s. The savings and loan industry, it is argued, was actually insolvent at the beginning of the decade, before the federal deregulation in the spring of 1980 and the fall of 1982. Furthermore, the industry's

4

insolvency at the time cannot be attributed to fraud and insider abuse. Instead, the rigid institutional design of savings and loans and the double-digit interest rates in the late 1970s and the early 1980s combined to drive the industry deep into insolvency. The governmental response to this situation only made matters worse when inadequately capitalized institutions were permitted to engage in high-risk activities in an effort to return to solvency or to reap huge returns on relatively little capital. Only with federal deposit insurance and under lax regulation and supervision could insolvent savings and loans gamble for resurrection and, more generally, inadequately capitalized institutions engage in high-risk activities. The delay in reorganizing or closing troubled institutions then permitted the ultimate resolution costs to grow so large that the government was not adequately protecting taxpayers.

Chapter 4 describes and evaluates the legislation passed by Congress and signed into law by President Bush in August 1989. That legislation was designed to resolve the savings and loan crisis and to prevent this situation from ever recurring. The legislation, however, reduces the value of the savings and loan charter, while not actually correcting the moral hazard inherent in the structure of the federal deposit insurance system. Although $50 billion was made available by this legislation to resolve insolvent savings and loans, the administration subsequently raised its estimate of the present-value cost of cleaning up the mess to between $89 and $132 billion in May 1990. Such enormous costs, which will be borne largely by taxpayers and which may be increased even more before this problem has been fully resolved, clearly dramatize the need to address the weaknesses in the last major piece of legislation affecting financial depository institutions enacted in the 1980s. We must then decide the most appropriate way in which to correct those weaknesses. After describing and assessing this legislation, the chapter considers the condition of the savings and loan industry and the actions taken by the Resolution Trust Corporation as the decade of the 1990s began.

Chapter 5 describes the structure of the federal deposit insurance system and the way in which the problem of moral hazard arises. Clearly, the current structure not only virtually eliminates depositor discipline but also exposes taxpayers to losses. Without depositor discipline, only two sources of discipline remain. The first comes from the owners of the depository institutions whose contributed equity capital is at risk. The more capital at risk, the greater the market discipline imposed by the owners. The second source of discipline comes from the government. The more appropriate the regulation and supervision are, the greater the discipline imposed by the government. It is argued, however, that competing forces are at work in a system in which both the government and the market impose discipline on federally insured institutions. Because it is ultimately liable for all losses, the government regulates and supervises the insured institutions to keep their losses under control and contained within the industry. At the same time, the owners are not collectively liable for all losses but instead liable only for their institution's losses to the limited extent of the owner-contributed equity capital and the losses of others to the limited extent of the accumulated insurance premiums levied upon the institution. Once the contributed equity capital of an owner has been depleted through his institution's losses and the losses of other institutions financed by the premiums, the government becomes liable for all remaining losses. Since owner-contributed equity capital imposes discipline, the government must reinforce that control by requiring adequate capital and reorganizing or closing undercapitalized institutions in a timely and cost-effective manner. If inadequate capital is tolerated, owners will have both the incentive and the opportunity for high-risk activities or for gambling for resurrection with federally insured deposits. But in imposing capital requirements upon insured depository institutions, the government must take into account the effects of regulations and supervision, since they bear directly on the profitability of institutions and their ability to attract equity capital. If the environment becomes so inflexible that insured institutions cannot adapt to changing market forces, other financial firms will come into existence and through competition worsen the situation for the insured institutions, although certainly improving the situation for consumers. To protect the taxpayer, the government must therefore structure federal deposit insurance to contain risk-taking behavior, while permitting activities sufficiently profitable to attract enough equity capital to levy the premiums necessary to cover any losses. This is a difficult and controversial task.

Chapter 6 focuses particularly on lessons that apply to all federally insured depository institutions. Most important, government regulation and supervision can themselves prevent and inhibit institutions from adapting to changing market forces. This tendency not only adversely affects their profitability and capitalization but also increases the risk exposure of the federal insurer and thus the taxpayer. As a result, deposit insurance cannot be properly reformed without also reforming the regulatory and supervisory environment within which insured depository institutions operate, an environment that was created largely in response to a completely different set of market forces during the 1930s.

2
Savings and Loans, 1830–1980

We have important lessons to learn from the long history of the savings and loan industry. The industry came into existence in the early years of our nation to fill a void: a group of private citizens organized an institution that specialized in financing home ownership. As is the case for all depository institutions, the problem was to obtain funds for loans or, more generally, to acquire assets and control losses. Since losses occur when assets decline in value, accurate information about the quality of assets, including any collateral for those assets, is needed; the assets must then be monitored so that timely and cost-effective actions can be taken when problems arise. Only in this way can assets be properly evaluated, priced, and monitored by an institution. At the same time, the liabilities incurred to fund the assets were of some concern. If liability holders decided to withdraw some of their funds, the timing could force the liquidation of assets at losses.

The early savings and loans attempted to minimize these potential problems in interesting ways. They were organized as mutual institutions, for example, which meant that any losses would be borne by the liability holders, who were also the owners. Those putting their savings into such institutions thus had an incentive to view the institution's liabilities as long-term debt rather than the demand debt issued by commercial banks at the time. The institutions produced relatively accurate information about the loans that were being made, since their directors and

NOTE: This chapter draws heavily on Barth and Regalia (1988).

managers were not only the owners but also the borrowers. Furthermore, this particular institutional arrangement and the restriction that homes so financed be located in the community kept the cost of producing information about the loans as well as monitoring them relatively low.

As market forces evolved, however, savings and loans were not able to adapt freely to their new and changing environment. First the state governments and then the federal government increasingly determined the institutional design of the savings and loan industry as it developed. Indeed, the disaster that struck the savings and loan industry in the 1980s was no historical accident but instead reflected the cumulative actions of the government to regulate and supervise savings and loans in an effort to promote home ownership.

The Early Years

The very first U.S. savings and loan institution, the Oxford Provident Building Association, was established in Frankford, Pennsylvania, on January 3, 1831. It was organized to pool the savings of individuals so that a subset of them could gain access to sufficient funds to acquire homes. Over the years, every individual was to be afforded the opportunity to borrow funds for this specific purpose, with the institution simply terminating after the last home loan had been made and repaid.

Oxford Provident Building Association was organized as a mutual institution, meaning that it was owned solely by those putting their savings into the institution or, as they were then known, shareholder members. Unlike an ordinary corporation, the association had no stockholders and thus no owner-contributed equity capital. So that accurate information about the quality of loans could be produced and the loans could be easily monitored, membership was geographically restricted, and loans were made only for homes within five miles of Frankford. Shareholders were expected to leave their funds with the institution throughout its life. Unlike owners of an ordinary corporation, however, those wishing to withdraw their shares were allowed to do so but only with a month's notice and a penalty payment of 5 percent of the amount withdrawn. These restrictions clearly signaled to potential members that Oxford Provident Building Association was a savings institution and not a commercial bank that facilitates the making of payments and permits the withdrawal of funds on demand. The balance sheet of the institution therefore consisted of home mortgage loans as assets and ownership shares as liabilities, with relatively little accumulated retained earnings or net worth. The term "shares" eventually was replaced by the term "savings accounts" and, more recently, after legislative approval, by the term "savings deposits." In certain key respects, the early savings and loans operated like modern day mutual funds.

The founders of the first savings and loan in the United States envisioned an institution that would operate only long enough to afford each shareholder the opportunity to own a home. The institution economized on information and transactions costs by consolidating the savings of a group of *local* individuals and rechanneling the funds to the same individuals in the form of home mortgage loans. This particular institutional design also imposed discipline on all the activities of the firm. Only years later did the institutional structure respond to the growth in population and income by severing the direct link between savers and borrowers. "Savings" and "loans" were then viewed more generally as joint but separable products offered by this particular type of institution. Thus, the first savings and loan was founded specifically to gather savings and to finance home ownership. More generally, long-term funds were used to acquire long-term assets, thereby minimizing any maturity mismatch problems. This early institution was a "narrow" savings and loan. The financing of home ownership was a specialized service not adequately provided by the other financial institutions in existence at the time.

No historical accident prevented commercial banks and mutual savings banks from engaging heavily in this particular activity. Although both types of financial institutions had been providing credit and issuing debt before savings and loans came into existence, neither catered to the home market. Unlike savings and loans, commercial banks were organized as stock institutions and issued debt payable on demand, such as notes that circulated as currency and demand deposits, both of which facilitated the payments system. This type of debt was acceptable to bank customers because it was backed by short-term commercial loans—and was thus fairly easy to value and monitor—and was senior to shareholder or owner-contributed equity capital in the event an institution became insolvent. Furthermore, commercial banks maintained relatively high though declining capital-to-asset ratios

10

throughout the 1800s and early 1900s. Indeed, as Wesley Lindow observes, "Early in the 1800's, the ratio of capital to total assets ranged around 60% and drifted down steadily thereafter. By the early 1900's this ratio had fallen to about 20% and the rapid expansion of bank assets during World War I and the 1920's pulled it down below 13%" (Lindow 1963, 30). Clearly, commercial banks were developing an informational comparative advantage in the early years of the United States by becoming directly involved in the payments system and catering to the short-term business loan market. They operated, in other words, as "narrow" banks. Mutual savings banks did not issue debt payable on demand but instead focused on the savings of the general public. Unlike savings and loans, however, they were originally philanthropic and their profits "were restricted to the amount of interest paid to deposits" (Summerfield 1960, 89). Since their intent was to provide a range of financial services to the small saver, the deposits at mutual savings banks had to be more flexible in both amounts and maturities. To minimize the losses on any forced sale of assets to provide this flexibility, a correspondingly much more flexible asset portfolio than home mortgages alone was required. All three types of depository institutions, therefore, were initially organized in different ways to specialize in a particular product market, and the specialization was reflected in the balance sheets of the institutions.

As savings and loans grew in number and spread throughout the nation, innovations in their design began to occur. Institutions began to operate on a perpetual basis, for example, and thus began to accept shareholder members who were not obliged to take out home mortgage loans. This development not only enlarged the pool of potential shareholders but also emphasized the strictly savings aspect of membership in an institution. Savings and loans, however, still generally did not issue deposits per se. Indeed, in many states, savings and loans were precluded by law from doing so. It was not until the advent of federal deposit insurance for savings and loans in the 1930s that deposits as such became widespread. Only then could individuals withdraw *exactly* the funds they had placed into an institution. At the same time, savings and loans ceased to operate like modern day mutual funds.

Accompanying the growth of the savings and loan industry during its first century were first state and then federal regulations. As the roles of saver and borrower became more distinct and separate and as the shareholders or owners became more numerous and less directly involved in management, the shareholder demand for outside regulation and supervision increased. The state governments, which were the only chartering agents for savings and loans until the 1930s, responded by imposing discipline on these early institutions. State requirements shifted part of the cost of producing information about the financial condition of institutions and monitoring their behavior from depositors to the state government.

State supervision evolved from reports to state officials, to permissive examinations by state officials, and then to required periodic examinations by state officials. In this way, states were able to show "their disapproval of loans for purposes not strictly within the building and loan field, which [was determined to be] the financing of single-family residences" (Bodfish 1931, 130). In addition, "A rather common power given to the state official in charge of the supervision of building and loan associations [was] that of refusing to grant charters where there [did] not seem to be a necessity for another building and loan" (Bodfish 1931, 129). Thus, the discipline imposed upon savings and loans was aimed not only at preventing and detecting fraud and insider abuse but also at restricting the lending activities of savings and loans to home mortgages and, more generally, limiting the amount of competition within the industry. This particular form of regulation and supervision clearly enhanced the value of a savings and loan charter and was reinforced by the low number of failures of savings and loans in their formative years.

The first serious failures in the industry occurred during the economic downturn of the 1890s. The result was the virtual elimination of the so-called national institutions, which developed in the 1880s by gathering deposits and making home mortgage loans nationwide through branch offices and the mail. Although the downturn of the 1890s adversely affected both national and local institutions, the local firms attributed their problems to the "improper" loan strategy and subsequent failures of the national institutions. Customers, it was claimed, were unable to distinguish between the two types of savings and loans during the panic of 1893, with the local institutions suffering mainly because of this informational imperfection.

The increased competition engendered by the national institutions contributed to the establishment of the U.S. League of Local Building and Loan Associations (the precursor to the U.S. League of Savings Institutions). This group, which became and remained very influential until the late 1980s, successfully lobbied the state legislatures to curb the activities of the national institutions—a move that eventually drove the nationals out of business and with them nearly a century-long nationwide diversification in home mortgage loans. The value of the *local* savings and loan charter, however, was enhanced by this action.

Although the local community savings and loans successfully eliminated competition from the national institutions, they increasingly encountered competition from commercial banks as the commercial banking industry attempted to adapt to changing market forces. Although commercial banks continued to specialize in financing business with demand deposits, the nature of business itself was changing in fundamental ways as the population increased and the economy grew throughout the nineteenth and into the twentieth centuries. Businesses became larger and serviced ever-wider geographical areas as transportation and technologies to produce and monitor information improved. These developments put more and more pressure on the commercial banks to expand their range of activities beyond demand deposits and short-term business loans. Consumer savings were growing, and businesses were demanding funds for land, buildings, and equipment. Investment capital, not just working capital, was being sought. The pressure was particularly intense for the local commercial banks, which were scattered throughout the country as individual units because nationwide branching was prohibited. These banks realized their continued existence depended on providing products to all members of the communities in which they were located, a situation clearly calling for more than short-term loans to commercial businesses. Typically state chartered, most local banks were able to obtain permission from the state authorities to increase their services. To remain competitive, federally chartered or national banks also sought permission to do likewise, although the activities generally emphasized were somewhat different, reflecting the larger size of the communities in which these institutions were located. Willis and Chapman observe, interestingly enough, that "lowering the minimum capital requirement in 1900 was the first important measure of the national banking system to meet the competition of state banks"

(Willis and Chapman 1934, 199). In return for their efforts, in the early 1900s national banks were no longer prohibited from accepting savings deposits. Moreover, commercial bank members of the Federal Reserve System now had an incentive to tap this particular source of funds when a lower reserve requirement was placed on savings deposits than on demand deposits. On the asset side, competition for home mortgages was also beginning to develop between savings and loans and commercial banks, but to a much lesser extent. Indeed, national banks, in fact, as Willis and Chapman (1934, 199) point out, were "forbidden to make loans against the security of real estate" before 1913, although "state banks everywhere could do so . . . and in most instances without any stipulated restrictions as to the amount of the loans, their duration, or the quality of the mortgages securing them." The two types of depository institutions found, however, that comparative advantages in loan information production and the associated monitoring process, as well as the favorable tax treatment afforded savings and loans, still led to fairly identifiable balance sheet differences.

Thus, as the economic boom of the 1920s began, the commercial banks and savings and loans still maintained different balance sheets, competed only partially, and were regulated to a different degree and by different levels of government. The federal regulators concentrated mostly on commercial banks because of their role in the payments mechanism, whereas the state governments focused on savings and loans and their role in facilitating home ownership and on state-chartered commercial banks and their ability to remain viable and to compete with the national banks.

The Great Depression Years

In only two periods in their first 150 years of existence have savings and loans suffered any significant number of failures or substantial failure costs: the first, the severe economic downturn of the 1890s and the second, the Great Depression.

During the 1930s, savings and loans did not issue liabilities payable on demand and therefore did not suffer the runs that plagued commercial banks. Nevertheless, they suffered withdrawals as their members drew upon their savings in an attempt to maintain consumption, and commercial banks drew down their accounts to obtain desperately needed liquidity. Savings and loans were hard pressed to meet these withdrawals because their assets consisted almost entirely of relatively illiquid home mortgage loans. Because they did not offer demand deposits, savings and loans had deliberately held very few liquid assets. Moreover, the net worth or capital at savings and loans was low because "many state laws . . . discouraged the accumulation of reserves and some supervisory authorities practically forced the distribution of all earnings" (Bodfish 1931, 7). As withdrawals mounted and assets declined in value because of the unprecedented number of real estate delinquencies and defaults, savings and loans experienced record failures. These failures during the 1930s not only inflicted severe losses on the shareholders or owners of savings and loans but also sharply curtailed the flow of funds into housing.

The disaster in the housing market brought about a new role for the federal government in this market, which included the way in which the savings and loan industry was regulated. First, on July 22, 1932, the Federal Home Loan Bank Act was signed by President Hoover. This act established the Federal Home Loan Bank System, consisting of twelve regional Federal Home Loan (FHL) banks under the supervision of the Federal Home Loan Bank Board (FHLBB). Originally an independent agency, the FHLBB was placed under other agencies from 1939 to 1955, at which time it regained its original status as an independent agency until abolished in October 1989. The main purpose of the new system was to give member savings and loans access to a reliable and steady source of funds during turbulent times to promote home ownership without disruptions. Member savings and loans, which were directly regulated only to a limited degree by the FHLBB, included all federal savings and loan institutions and those state-chartered institutions that voluntarily chose to become members and qualified for membership. The system was designed so that the FHL banks could issue consolidated obligations in the capital markets and thus be able to advance funds to member savings and loans at low interest rates. Each of the FHL banks was established as a separate corporation privately owned by stockholders (the member savings and loans). It was stated at the time the system was established that "the Federal Home Loan Bank System . . . [was] not intended to 'bail out' embarrassed financial institutions" and that "the dealings of the bank must be

15

confined to institutions that are solvent and reasonably safe credit risks" (Bodfish and Theobald 1940, 301).

Second, the Home Owners' Loan Act was signed on June 13, 1933, to allow the newly established FHLBB, the precursor to the Office of Thrift Supervision, to charter and regulate the operations of federal savings and loans. The apparent rationale for the chartering of federal institutions was that these institutions are less prone to financial difficulties than state institutions, as evidenced by their better performance over time. More specifically, of all depositors' losses in suspended commercial banks from 1865 to 1934, national banks accounted for $1.1 billion, whereas state banks accounted for $2.3 billion (see *Annual Report*, FDIC 1934, 90). At the time federally chartered savings and loans were also perceived to provide for those localities where the service of the state institutions was insufficient. Like state-chartered savings and loans, the federal institutions were required by the FHLBB to operate under mutual-type ownership and to service only customers in their local communities. The federal government, like the state governments before it, adhered to a policy of restricted geographical competition among savings and loans to enhance the value of the local charter.

Although the main purpose of the Home Owners' Loan Act was to facilitate the refinancing of existing mortgages in distress cases, many persons merely seeking the more favorable interest rate and other terms offered by the federal government were also able to obtain loans. Ironically, this desire to qualify for government loans on favorable terms caused many borrowers to default deliberately on their existing loans, thus aggravating the problems of savings and loans.

Finally, Title IV of the National Housing Act, which was enacted on June 27, 1934, created the Federal Savings and Loan Insurance Corporation (FSLIC), the precursor to the Savings Association Insurance Fund, to provide federal insurance for deposits at savings and loans. The FSLIC was administered by the FHLBB, with compulsory membership for federal institutions and optional membership for state-chartered institutions. Insured institutions were subject to FHLBB regulations regarding the geographical area in which loans could be made, advertising and sales plans, and capital requirements. With the establishment of the FSLIC, the savings and loans had equal footing with commercial banks, whose deposits were insured by the Federal Deposit Insurance Corporation (FDIC), including both demand and savings deposits.

Postwar Growth and Diversification

Following the Great Depression and World War II, savings and loans grew tremendously for nearly four decades. They surpassed mutual savings banks in total assets for the first time in 1954 and grew to half the size of commercial banks by the end of 1980. This dramatic expansion occurred throughout the entire industry for both large and small institutions.

The magnitude of the redistribution of total financial assets over this period was quite remarkable. As table 2–1 shows, financial assets held by all financial service firms in 1945 totaled $247 billion. Of this amount, savings and loans held a meager 3 percent, compared with 65 percent for commercial banks. By 1980, however, savings and loans had increased their share of the total to 15 percent, while the share for commercial banks had declined to only 37 percent. Mutual savings banks and life insurance companies (insurance companies from the 1930s on) also lost considerable ground during this period. Moreover, although the share of total financial assets accounted for by all the depository financial service firms declined to 58 percent from 76 percent, the share of savings and loans quintupled.

The relative growth in savings and loans is even more impressive considering the increased competition among the different types of financial service firms. In the late 1950s and 1960s, more than half the deposits in commercial banks were non-interest-bearing demand deposits. By the late 1970s, however, this relatively low-cost source of funds accounted for only about one-fourth of commercial bank deposits. In contrast, time and passbook savings accounts at savings and loans accounted for about the same 75 to 80 percent of total deposits over the time period. They were, moreover, prohibited by law from even offering demand deposits. The commercial banks were therefore finding it increasingly necessary to compete heavily for the main source of funds for savings and loans, even though savings and loans had not yet received unrestricted permission to vie for what had historically been the main source of funds for commercial banks.

In addition to the accelerated competition from other de-

17

TABLE 2–1
Percentage of Total U.S. Financial Assets Held by Financial Service Firms, 1900–1980

	1900	1929	1933	1945	1955	1965	1975	1980
Commercial banks	66	60	51	65	44	36	37	37
Savings and loans	3	7	7	3	9	14	16	15
Mutual savings banks	16	9	12	7	8	6	6	4
Credit unions	—[b]	—[b]	—[b]	1	1	1	2	2
Life insurance companies	12	16	23	18	21	17	13	12
Other institutions[a]	3	8	7	6	17	26	26	30
Total assets (billions of dollars)	15	110	90	247	424	921	2,136	4,032

a. Includes such financial intermediaries as private pension funds, state and local government retirement funds, finance companies, other insurance companies, and money market mutual funds, and mutual funds.
b. Less than 1.
SOURCE: Barth and Regalia (1988).

pository institutions for the savings of consumers, some nondepository and hence less regulated financial firms responded to the
market forces of the time by offering small savers a product that
better protected them against inflation and high interest rates.
The laws and regulations had prohibited depository institutions
from paying interest on demand deposits since the 1930s and had
limited the rates of interest and maturities that could be offered
on savings and time deposits since 1966. As a result, savings and
loans and other depository institutions were finding it difficult to
compete for funds with the less regulated nondepository financial
firms that could offer higher interest rates and more flexible maturities. Thus, even access to federally insured deposits was an
insufficient competitive edge for depository institutions as informational technologies and the economic environment were
undergoing rapid and significant change.

This interaction between market interest rates and regulatory constraints led to the development of money market mutual
funds in the early 1970s. The institutional design of this type of
financial service firm was successful because it was not con-
strained by regulation of the type of products offered and their
pricing. Customers were attracted by the offer of a new type of
account paying higher interest than other financial depository service firms could pay and offering limited check-writing privileges.
By the late 1970s, these money market funds, with their highly
liquid assets to match their shorter-term liabilities, had grown
large enough to be a serious competitive threat to depository financial institutions. This threat spurred the development and regulatory approval of new market-based deposits that could be offered by depository institutions, such as the six-month money
market certificate in June 1978, whose rate of interest was tied
to the six-month Treasury bill rate, the small saver certificates
in January 1980, and money market deposit accounts in December
1982.

Moreover, in response to the unattractiveness of demand
deposits paying no explicit interest, the depository institutions
created interest-bearing checking accounts as direct substitutes
for demand deposits. These new accounts were first introduced
in Massachusetts in 1972, spreading to six other northeastern
states by the mid-1970s before Congress authorized them for nationwide use in 1981 by commercial banks, savings and loans,
mutual savings banks, and credit unions.

19

Although the 1970s marked the beginning of what became extensive changes on the liability side of the balance sheet for depository institutions, only in the 1980s was the asset side permitted to catch up with the changes. More specifically, as savings and loans were offering higher rates to retain and attract funds, the use to which they could put those funds was still restricted largely to home mortgages. To compound this problem, in 1974 Congress rejected variable-rate mortgages, which had existed in the early 1970s in such states as Wisconsin and California, on a national basis. Although federally chartered savings and loans were allowed to issue variable-rate mortgages in those few states where state-chartered institutions were permitted to do so, only in the early 1980s were all federally chartered savings and loans allowed to offer adequately designed variable-rate mortgages to help insulate them from adverse movements in interest rates.

Besides the more widely known laws and regulations that restricted the ability of institutions to modify their design in response to changing market forces, the federal tax code also provided an incentive for savings and loans to specialize in home mortgages. Until the Revenue Act of 1951, savings and loans were exempt from federal income taxes. Although this act terminated their tax-exempt status, savings and loans could nonetheless avoid paying taxes because up to 100 percent of their taxable income was deductible through the establishment of a bad debt reserve. In 1962, however, the bad debt deduction was reduced to 60 percent of taxable income, subject to a qualifying asset restriction. This restriction stated that for a savings and loan to be eligible for the maximum deduction, 82 percent or more of its assets had to consist of cash, U.S. government securities, passbook loans, and one-to-four family residential property loans. The bad debt deduction was reduced by three quarters of one percentage point for every 1 percent the qualified assets fell below 82 percent of total assets, with no deduction if these assets fell below 60 percent.

The Tax Reform Act of 1969 modified this restriction by permitting a savings and loan to base its bad debt deduction on taxable income, loan loss experience, or percentage of eligible loans. Since the vast majority of institutions used the taxable income method, the deduction was reduced in scheduled steps from 60 percent of taxable income in 1969 to 40 percent in 1979. The Tax Equity and Fiscal Responsibility Act of 1982 further reduced the bad debt deduction to 34 percent in 1982 and then to 32 percent in 1984. More recently, the Tax Reform Act of 1986 reduced the bad debt deduction as a percentage of taxable income to 8 percent in 1987. To be eligible for the maximum deduction, a savings and loan had to have only 60 percent or more of its assets in qualifying assets. Thus, over time, the federal tax laws offered a large incentive, although diminishing in recent years, for savings and loans to concentrate their investments in home mortgages.

In sum, various laws and regulations have influenced the institutional design of a savings and loan by limiting lending to local home mortgage loans, which for years meant loans secured by houses within 50 miles of an institution's home office, and by limiting the issuance of liabilities almost entirely to savings deposits. Indeed, only in 1964 were federal institutions permitted to make unsecured, personal loans for college or educational expenses—the first time they had been allowed to make loans for any purpose other than acquiring real estate. In the same year, the geographical limit for mortgage loans was extended to 100 miles, and up to 5 percent could be lent in large metropolitan areas outside this limit. In later years Congress extended this limit to encompass an institution's home state—and beyond that for the largest savings and loans. Then, in 1983, the FHLBB permitted federal institutions to make loans nationwide. Unless prohibited by state law, state institutions with FSLIC insurance could do the same. In 100 years, the savings and loan industry had come full circle—nationals were once again alive and well.

In 1964 federal institutions were also permitted to issue mortgages and buy property in urban renewal areas and to buy securities issued by federal, state, and municipal governments. In 1968, moreover, these institutions were allowed to make loans for mobile homes, second or vacation homes, and housing fixtures. Federal savings and loans could issue notes, bonds, and most other types of securities except capital stock. Thus began the savings and loans' entry into business areas long viewed as the exclusive domain of commercial banks. Yet, government regulation determined the evolution of the savings and loans as they adapted to changing market forces. By most accounts, the pace was unacceptably slow. Indeed, as early as 1961, the Commission on Money and Credit recommended that savings and loans be given greater flexibility in their asset portfolios. The merit in this recommendation was evident when in 1966 the profits of savings and loans were badly squeezed as interest rates reached their highest level in many years. As savings and loans suffered losses and large withdrawals, they

> toyed with the idea of creating an agency that would buy mortgages from S&L's to give them extra cash during tight-money periods . . . and considered variable-rate mortgages that have higher interest rates in tight-money periods and allow S&L's to raise savings account rates without getting squeezed by low mortgage returns. However, the FHLBB did not think that these plans were practical, so they were scrapped (Marvell 1969, 234–35).

Instead, the savings and loan industry sought to obtain the power to make more short-term loans and to issue more long-term liabilities. One possible way to achieve this goal was to convert to savings banks, most of which already had the power to issue long-term notes. Furthermore, while most of their loans were mortgages, in the mid-1960s 25 percent were generally in short-term investments, as compared with 15 percent for savings and loans and 85 percent for commercial banks. The problem was that only eighteen states chartered savings banks and federal charters were unavailable to this type of depository institution. An attempt was therefore made to get Congress to give federal charters to savings banks and allow savings and loans to convert to savings banks. Although Presidents Kennedy and Johnson as well as various members of Congress supported broader asset diversification powers for federally chartered savings institutions, the only progress was a 1968 bill that permitted federal savings and loans to lend money for housing fixtures and to call their savings shares or accounts "savings deposits," a commercial banking term that the savings and loan industry had wanted to use because it suggested security to many people and would therefore help attract more savings. Furthermore, savings and loans were permitted to issue notes and bonds to supplement savings deposits as sources of funds. Recognizing that the basic problem of savings and loans had not really been corrected—being short-term borrowers and long-term lenders—in 1972 the Hunt Commission recommended that savings institutions be given the necessary authority to compete more fully with commercial banks in order to survive. Three years later, the House Banking Committee commissioned a comprehensive study of the U.S. financial system entitled "Financial Institutions and the Nation's Economy," more commonly referred to as the FINE study. The study recommended broader powers for savings institutions, and the subsequent proposed legislation would have expanded the range of activities in which savings and loans could engage. As pointed out by Raymond Natter (undated mimeo), "In testifying in favor of the legislation, the Federal Home Loan Bank Board noted 'the pressing need for restructuring of our financial institutions to bring their asset and liability powers into better alignment with the financial market realities of our modern economy.'" The subsequent legislation enacted in 1978 limited sharply the permissible diversification of savings and loans. More significant legislative and administrative efforts at deregulating savings and loans as well as the other depository institutions culminated in legislation in 1980 and 1982. At the signing ceremony of the 1980 legislation, President Carter, as Raymond Natter points out, stated that "under existing law, which this bill will change, our banks and savings institutions are hampered by a wide range of outdated, unfair, and unworkable regulations" (undated mimeo).

The entire administrative and congressional history of efforts to broaden the powers of savings and loans, presented in appendix A, demonstrates that during the twenty years before 1980 the highly rigid design of these institutions was well known. The financial problems they encountered in 1966, 1969–1970, and 1973–1974, although short-lived, had clearly signaled that this was indeed the case. Not until the early 1980s, however, was major legislation enacted belatedly attempting to allow savings and loans to catch up with the realities of the private marketplace. Chapter 3 documents how market forces ravaged the government-regulated and-supervised savings and loan industry and how the actions of the government actually worsened rather than diminished the problems.

3
The Turbulent 1980s

Until the 1980s, most persons viewed the savings and loan industry as sleepy and uneventful. To be sure, people knew of occasional serious problems, like those that hit the industry hard in the 1890s and the 1930s. But it was generally assumed those problems were forever behind us. After all, the purpose of all the legislation enacted during the Great Depression was to insulate the public—and, as part of this process, the savings and loans— once and for all from such severe disruptions. As discussed earlier, this protection of the savings and loans was to be accomplished through federal regulation and supervision to contain and monitor risk taking; through federal deposit insurance to keep any losses within the industry; and through FHL banks as an additional and relatively low-cost source of funds to savings and loans during stressful periods.

Despite the entirely new regulatory and supervisory apparatus, however, savings and loans were devastated in the 1980s, more so than in the 1890s and, more surprisingly, more so even than in the 1930s (see Barth and Regalia 1988, 126–27). Indeed, the problems in this industry have produced the biggest financial disaster in modern history. It is important to explain what happened and why it happened during this period unprecedented in U.S. financial history.

An Overview of the Savings and Loan Industry

A fairly complete picture of the savings and loan industry during the 1980s is provided by the information presented in table 3–1.

NOTE: This chapter draws heavily on Barth, Bartholomew, and Labich (1989) and Barth and Bradley (1989).

TABLE 3-1: SAVINGS AND LOAN INDUSTRY, 1980–1989

	1980	1981	1982	1983	1984	1985	1986	1987	1988	1989
Number of institutions	3,993	3,751	3,287	3,146	3,136	3,246	3,220	3,147	2,949	2,878
Total assets ($ billions)	604	640	686	814	978	1,070	1,164	1,251	1,352	1,252
GAAP net worth ($ billions)	32	27	20	25	27	34	39	34	46	25
Tangible net worth ($ billions)	32	25	4	4	3	9	15	9	23	10
Net income ($ millions)	781	(4,631)	(4,142)	1,945	1,022	3,728	131	(7,779)	(12,057)	(19,172)
Net operating income ($ millions)	790	(7,114)	(8,761)	(46)	990	3,601	4,562	2,850	907	(2,913)
Net nonoperating income ($ millions)	298	964	3,041	2,567	796	2,215	(1,290)	(7,930)	(11,012)	(15,449)
Taxes ($ millions)	407	(1,519)	(1,578)	576	764	2,087	3,141	2,699	1,952	800
Percentage of home mortgages to total assets	66.5	65.0	56.3	49.8	44.9	42.4	38.9	37.8	38.6	40.7

(Table 3–1 continues)

25

TABLE 3–1 (continued)

	1980	1981	1982	1983	1984	1985	1986	1987	1988	1989
Percentage of mortgage backed securities to total assets	4.4	5.0	8.6	10.9	11.1	10.4	13.1	15.6	15.4	13.7
Percentage of mortgage assets to total assets	70.9	70.0	64.9	60.7	56.0	52.8	52.0	53.4	54.0	54.4
Stock institutions										
Percentage of number of institutions	20.0	21.0	23.0	24.0	30.0	33.0	37.0	40.0	44.0	43.0
Percentage of total assets	27.0	29.0	30.0	40.0	52.0	56.0	62.0	70.0	74.0	71.0
Federally chartered										
Percentage of number of institutions	50.0	51.0	51.0	51.0	54.0	53.0	54.0	56.0	58.0	62.0
Percentage of total assets	56.0	63.0	70.0	66.0	64.0	64.0	64.0	65.0	71.0	76.0

26

TAP capital-to-asset
ratio

<0%										
Number	43	112	415	515	695	705	672	672	508	517
Total TAP-assets ($ billions)	0.4	29	220	234	336	335	324	336	283	283
0% to 1.5%										
Number	63	178	291	310	327	266	227	194	160	122
Total TAP-assets ($ billions)	4	50	81	88	153	135	144	143	182	60
1.5% to 3%										
Number	230	524	592	569	526	460	354	277	281	245
Total TAP-assets ($ billions)	39	113	136	185	168	212	191	196	244	206
3% to 6%										
Number	1,956	1,766	1,202	1,091	945	1,009	995	891	864	814
Total TAP-assets ($ billions)	379	348	190	222	227	259	316	356	418	480
>6%										
Number	1,701	1,171	787	661	643	806	972	1,113	1,136	1,180
Total TAP-assets ($ billions)	181	101	59	84	62	95	156	188	196	206

(Table 3–1 continues)

27

TABLE 3–1 (continued)

	1980	1981	1982	1983	1984	1985	1986	1987	1988	1989
Resolutions										
Number	11	28	63	36	22	30	46	47	205	37
Total assets ($ millions)	1,458	13,908	17,662	4,631	5,080	5,601	12,455	10,660	100,660	9,662
Estimated present-value cost ($ millions)	167	759	803	275	743	979	3,065	3,704	31,180	5,608

NOTE: Data for 1989 are for all thrifts. At year-end, there were 281 institutions in conservatorship with assets of $92.6 billion. Resolutions in 1988 do not include eighteen "stabilizations" that had assets of $7,463 million and tangible net worth of negative $3,348 million, and an estimated present-value resolution cost of $6,838 million. Resolutions in 1989 do not include seven FSLIC resolutions (reportedly at no cost to FSLIC) and two Resolution Trust Corporation resolutions (reportedly at no cost to the corporation).
SOURCE: Federal Home Loan Bank Board and Office of Thrift Supervision.

A number of striking facts are revealed. First, the industry has been undergoing major consolidation since 1980. In that year, savings and loans numbered nearly 4,000, declining to just under 2,900 by the end of 1989. Included in this nearly 30 percent decline were 525 failed institutions that imposed an estimated present-value cost of nearly $50 billion upon the FSLIC. Total assets, however, increased to $1.3 trillion from $604 billion over the same period. Yet, despite this increase, the industry actually began to shrink at the end of the decade, as total assets diminished by $100 million in 1989. This shrinkage was caused by the resolution of insolvent savings and loans and the shedding of assets by institutions struggling to meet newly imposed and higher capital requirements. Second, the ownership structure of the industry has dramatically changed as stock rather than mutual institutions have become increasingly dominant. At the beginning of the decade, only 20 percent of all savings and loans were stockholder owned, with just 27 percent of total industry assets. By year end 1989, however, these savings and loans accounted for 43 percent of all institutions and held 71 percent of all assets. Third, while the percentage of federally chartered institutions increased by twelve percentage points to 62 percent from 1980 to 1989, the share of assets controlled by these institutions rose by twenty percentage points to 76 percent over the same period. This recent development and the legislation enacted in August 1989 clearly weaken the dual-charter system for the savings and loan industry and, more generally, raise questions about the future of the state charter for financial depository institutions. In 1990, however, some savings and loans wanted to convert to a state savings bank charter to eliminate the costs associated with regulation by the Office of Trust Supervision, and some state legislatures enacted the necessary legislation. Fourth, savings and loans have significantly diversified into new activities during this period as a result of state and federal deregulation. The share of assets devoted to home mortgages declined by a steep twenty-six percentage points—to 41 percent in 1989 from 67 percent in 1980. At the same time, the growing importance of the securitization of home mortgages is evident. Whereas savings and loans held only 4 percent of their assets in mortgage-backed securities in 1980, the share increased to 14 percent by 1989. This dramatic change makes it clear that developments in informational technology and the creation of secondary markets have rendered the origination, servicing, and holding of loans distinct and separable activities. Fifth, the industry lost a record $19 billion in 1989. Most of this loss was due to nonoperating factors (that is, asset write-downs and additions to loan loss reserves), reflecting a deterioration in asset quality. In contrast, the nearly $9 billion lost in 1981 and 1982 resulted entirely from operating factors (that is, a negative interest rate spread), reflecting adverse movements in interest rates. Stated another way, savings and loans faced an interest rate problem in the early 1980s and an asset quality problem in the latter part of the decade. These loss figures clearly indicate that the savings and loan industry was in deep trouble long before President Bush took office in early 1989 and shortly thereafter stated that taxpayers would be required to share in the burden of cleaning up the savings and loan mess. Sixth, the number of tangible-insolvent savings and loans—the most conservative or strictest accounting measure of the capital of an institution—increased each year until 1985. Even though the number declined for the next several years, 517 institutions were insolvent but still operating with $283 billion in assets at yearend 1989. The existence of these institutions and the hundreds of others that were reporting inadequate capital explains why the savings and loan problem was far from being resolved at the end of the decade. Finally, the number of institutions with tangible capital-to-asset ratios exceeding 6 percent—which was roughly where the industry reported itself at the beginning of the 1980s—has actually been increasing since 1984. At yearend 1989, however, there were only 1,180 such savings and loans, holding a relatively paltry $206 billion in assets.

Failures and Resolutions

Hundreds of savings and loans failed and were resolved by the FSLIC—the precursor to the Resolution Trust Corporation—during the 1980s. The terms "failure" and "resolution," however, have not always been clear. Failure occurs when a savings and loan no longer has any positive owner-contributed equity capital. Determining precisely when such capital has been depleted is typically difficult and controversial for federally insured institutions, however, particularly in the case of institutions with mutual-type ownership.

Despite this problem (which may sometimes be exaggerated insofar as Benston, Carhill, and Olasov [1990] find "that even a very generic market-valuation is superior to traditional accounting methodologies" [p 35]), information regarding accounting or book value measures of capital is readily available. One can determine, for example, the number of institutions that are tangible-insolvent. Whether the FSLIC took an action against an insolvent institution and if that action required an expenditure or commitment of funds can also be determined. The minimum total failures during the 1980s can be approximated by adding the number of savings and loans against which the FSLIC took action to the number of open but tangible-insolvent institutions.

The FSLIC took five different types of actions against insolvent institutions from 1980 through 1989: (1) liquidation; (2) assisted merger; (3) stabilization; (4) management consignment program (MCP); and (5) supervisory merger. Liquidation and assisted merger, generally referred to as resolutions, were meant to be final and to impose costs on the FSLIC. A supervisory merger was also meant to be final but not to impose cost on the FSLIC. Stabilization and the MCP were temporary actions that would eventually be followed by liquidations or mergers.

As table 3–2 shows, the FSLIC liquidated 78 institutions, engaged in 411 assisted mergers, 77 MCPs, 18 stabilizations, and 333 supervisory mergers from 1980 through 1988. The estimated present-value cost of the liquidations, assisted mergers, and stabilizations was nearly $50 billion. These institutions collectively held $180 billion in assets. In 1988 alone, 223 thrifts were resolved or stabilized at an estimated cost of $38 billion. (The FDIC was required by law to reassess the cost of these transactions, which resulted in the estimated present-value cost being increased to $47 billion in August 1990.) Although the FSLIC took action against a greater number of troubled savings and loans in 1982, most were supervisory mergers, and the estimated cost was only $803 million.

Mainly as a result of all the actions taken in 1988, the number of tangible-insolvent institutions declined to 508 at the end of the year from 672 in the previous year (see table 3–1). These institutions held $283 billion in assets. Adding together insolvent and other nearly insolvent institutions, in congressional testimony in March 1989 the FHLBB identified 578 savings and loans that would likely require future action at an estimated present-value

31

TABLE 3–2: ATTRITION AMONG FEDERALLY INSURED SAVINGS

	Failed					
	FSLIC assistance					
	Liquidations			Mergers and other types of assisted resolutions		
	Number	Total assets[a]	Total cost[a]	Number	Total assets[a]	Total cost[a,b]
1934–79	13	349	16	130	4,110	290
1980	0	0	0	11	1,458	167
1981	1	89	30	27	13,820	728
1982	1	36	3	62	17,626	800
1983	5	263	61	31	4,369	214
1984	9	1,498	583	13	3,583	159
1985	9	2,141	630	22	4,227	392
1986	10	584	254	36	11,871	2,811
1987	17	3,044	2,278	30	7,617	1,426
1988	26	2,965	2,832	179	97,695	28,348
Total	91	10,969	6,687	541	166,376	35,335

NA = not applicable.
a. In millions of dollars.
b. These figures represent the estimated present-value cost of resolution at the time.

cost of $38 billion (see M. D. Wall 1989). These cost estimates of the FHLBB were a source of considerable controversy.

When newly elected President Bush announced on February 6, 1989, his plan to resolve once and for all the problems in the savings and loan industry, the resolution of troubled institutions virtually ground to a halt. Not until the Resolution Trust Corporation was established on August 9 of that year did the resolution process resume, although at a disappointingly slow pace. As a result of abolishing the FSLIC and establishing the corporation to resolve insolvent institutions, 1989 was essentially a lost year. As table 3–1 shows, only thirty-seven institutions were resolved in the entire year despite the hundreds of open institutions reporting insolvency.

AND LOAN INSTITUTIONS, 1934–1988

	Institutions				
	No FSLIC assistance				
Management consignment cases	Supervisory mergers	Nonfailed Institutions (voluntary mergers)	Total Attrition	All Institutions Total number	Total assets[d]
0	NA	NA	143	NA	NA
0	21	63	95	3,993	604
0	54	215	297	3,751	640
0	184	215	462	3,287	686
0	34	83	153	3,146	814
0	14	31	67	3,136	978
23	10	47	111	3,246	1,070
29	5	45	125	3,220	1,164
25	5	74	151	3,147	1,251
18[b]	6	25	254	2,949	1,352
95	333	798	1,858	NA	NA

c. Stabilizations: estimated total present-value cost of about $7 billion.
d. In billions of dollars.
SOURCE: Barth and Bradley (1989).

Regional Distribution of Resolution Costs

Table 3–3 shows that the distribution of the estimated present-value costs to resolve insolvent savings and loans during the 1980s, both across the country and over time, has been extremely uneven. The cost figures include only liquidations and assisted mergers, not the estimated $7 billion cost of the eighteen stabilizations in 1988. Clearly, Texas has by far accounted for the largest share—about half—of the total cost of all resolutions from 1980 through 1988. California, Florida, and Illinois together account for about another fourth of the total cost. Such information has led some to argue that the tax burden for cleaning up the savings and loan mess should reflect the regional distribution of

TABLE 3–3
ESTIMATED RESOLUTION COST OF SAVINGS AND LOAN FAILURES BY STATE, 1980–1988
(millions of dollars)

	1980	1981	1982	1983	1984	1985	1986	1987	1988	Total
Alabama	0	3	0	0	0	0	4	2	0	9
Alaska	0	0	0	3	0	0	0	0	13	16
Arizona	0	0	0	0	0	0	0	0	0	0
Arkansas	0	0	0	0	0	82	657	90	28	857
California	0	0	3	0	330	8	159	715	5,438	6,653
Colorado	0	0	0	0	0	22	36	0	585	643
Connecticut	0	0	0	0	0	0	0	0	0	0
Delaware	0	0	0	0	0	0	0	0	0	0
District of Columbia	0	3	0	0	0	62	0	0	0	65
Florida	15	33	16	0	0	15	701	0	1,325	2,105
Georgia	0	0	2	0	0	0	0	0	5	7
Hawaii	1	0	0	0	0	3	0	0	0	4
Idaho	0	0	0	0	0	0	0	121	2	123
Illinois	17	76	354	32	37	3	16	173	1,502	2,210
Indiana	0	0	0	38	0	0	0	0	145	183
Iowa	3	0	0	9	0	10	0	102	329	453
Kansas	0	0	3	0	0	8	7	20	20	58
Kentucky	0	0	8	0	0	16	93	0	84	201
Louisiana	0	0	3	21	4	65	418	539	177	1,227

										Total
Maine	0	0	0	0	0	0	0	0	0	0
Maryland	0	24	10	0	21	0	0	69	0	124
Massachusetts	0	0	51	0	0	0	0	0	0	51
Michigan	11	0	0	16	0	0	13	14	175	229
Minnesota	0	95	1	0	0	0	0	0	205	301
Mississippi	0	0	1	0	8	3	0	0	0	12
Missouri	0	51	1	77	0	0	75	100	0	304
Montana	0	0	5	0	0	5	0	0	11	21
Nebraska	0	0	0	0	0	0	0	5	0	5
Nevada	0	0	0	0	0	0	0	0	0	0
New Hampshire	0	0	0	0	0	0	0	0	0	0
New Jersey	10	9	21	0	16	0	0	55	230	341
New Mexico	2	0	2	6	0	5	2	0	80	97
New York	0	361	211	13	4	0	59	0	0	648
North Carolina	0	5	0	0	0	0	0	0	34	39
North Dakota	0	13	4	0	39	0	0	0	0	56
Ohio	104	0	0	27	28	2	222	22	451	856
Oklahoma	0	0	0	0	0	0	71	41	502	614
Oregon	0	0	0	0	0	146	21	27	362	556
Pennsylvania	0	0	11	13	0	0	0	0	0	24
Puerto Rico	0	84	7	0	1	0	0	0	0	92
Rhode Island	3	0	0	0	10	0	0	0	0	13

(Table 3-3 continues)

TABLE 3-3 (continued)

	1980	1981	1982	1983	1984	1985	1986	1987	1988	Total
South Carolina	0	0	0	0	0	0	0	0	0	0
South Dakota	0	0	0	4	0	0	0	0	8	12
Tennessee	0	0	0	0	80	17	0	0	34	131
Texas	0	1	78	0	164	155	493	1,504	19,491	21,886
Utah	0	0	0	0	0	163	0	46	0	209
Vermont	0	0	0	0	0	0	0	0	0	0
Virginia	0	0	14	12	1	18	0	35	136	216
Washington	0	0	0	0	0	174	(13)	22	92	275
Wisconsin	0	0	0	3	0	0	0	0	0	3
West Virginia	0	0	0	0	0	0	0	0	81	81
Wyoming	0	0	0	0	0	0	30	0	147	177
Total	166	758	805	275	743	982	3,064	3,702	31,692	42,187

SOURCE: Federal Home Loan Bank Board.

36

these resolution costs. It must be remembered, however, that many of the seriously troubled institutions were offering relatively high rates on their deposits and attracting them through the use of brokers from around the country. (The amount of broker-originated deposits increased to $71.7 billion at year-end 1988 from $1.7 billion at year-end 1979 and accounted for 0.4 and 7.4 percent of total deposits, respectively.) Individuals outside the regions in which the most troubled savings and loans were located were thus benefiting from the high deposit rates they were being paid. Furthermore, those persons with fixed-rate home mortgage loans at below-market rates reaped substantial benefits when the savings and loans lost money paying market rates on their deposits to fund those loans. By promoting home ownership as it did, the government benefited the home buyer at the expense of the savings and loans. More important, the regional argument regarding the allocation of resolution costs ignores the national commitment to protect all insured depositors when failures occur, a commitment to be fulfilled like all other such commitments.

Causes of the Debacle

At least eight factors can be identified as causes of the savings and loan debacle. Only by identifying and understanding the causes of this disaster can we determine the reforms necessary to prevent something similar from occurring in the future.

A Rigid Institutional Design. Since their origin in 1831, savings and loans have concentrated on gathering savings deposits and providing home mortgage loans. Until the 1980s, these institutions relied almost exclusively on savings deposits and invested nearly all these deposits in traditional home mortgages. As has already been documented, however, this particular decision on portfolio allocation was not made simply on the basis of normal market forces; for savings and loans have long been subjected to specific regulatory constraints regarding the assets they could hold and the liabilities they could issue. Moreover, regulations have governed the pricing of the institutions' products (for example, fixed as opposed to flexible interest rates on home mortgages and maximum interest rates on savings deposits), the geographical areas in which they could branch and make loans, the maturities they could offer depositors, and the extent to which they could engage in options and futures activities. Furthermore, the tax code provided an incentive to invest heavily in specific assets.

Thus, before the 1980s, savings and loan institutions were essentially required to specialize in gathering deposits to fund home mortgages and to price these products rigidly, despite the clear signals sent by changing market forces—that is, the informational and economic environment in which they operated. The profits savings and loans earned were, therefore, determined mainly by the extent to which the interest rate earned on home mortgages exceeded the interest rate paid on deposits, net of general and administrative expenses. The fixed mortgage rate combined with a variable deposit rate set the stage for a monumental disaster in a marketplace characterized by high and volatile interest rates. Thus, the rigidity of the institutional design was one cause of the savings and loan debacle.

High and Volatile Interest Rates. In the late 1970s and early 1980s, interest rates rose to unexpectedly high levels and became extremely volatile. Contributing to the large fluctuations in nominal interest rates were inflationary expectations and actions taken by the Board of Governors of the Federal Reserve System in the fall of 1979 to dampen those expectations. The sharp movements in interest rates severely affected the financial condition of the savings and loan industry. When interest rates skyrocketed in late 1979 and the early 1980s, net operating income plummeted (see table 3–1). Indeed, 85 percent of all savings and loans were unprofitable in 1981, and virtually all were insolvent if one had marked-to-market their fixed-rate residential mortgage loan portfolios. As table 3–4 shows, the three major accounting measures of capital for the industry all declined in 1981 and fell even more in 1982, with the strictest or most conservative measure declining the most (the note to table 3–4 describes the three different measures). On a market-value basis, the entire industry was deeply insolvent in 1981 and even in 1980 before any of the accounting measures of capital revealed the seriousness of the problem (see also Brumbaugh 1988; and Kane 1985 and 1989). As interest rates subsequently declined, net operating income and the market-value of the fixed-rate mortgage loan portfolio significantly improved, so that the market-value measure of capital became positive in 1985 and remained so into 1988. With liabilities repricing

TABLE 3-4

ALTERNATIVE CAPITAL-TO-ASSET RATIOS FOR THE SAVINGS AND LOAN INDUSTRY, 1980–1988

	1980	1981	1982	1983	1984	1985	1986	1987	1988
Regulatory accounting practices capital (RAP)	5.3	4.4	3.8	4.1	3.8	4.4	4.6	4.1	4.4
Generally accepted accounting principles capital (GAAP)	5.3	4.2	2.9	3.1	2.8	3.2	3.4	2.7	3.4
Tangible capital (TAP)	5.3	3.9	0.6	0.5	0.3	0.8	1.3	0.7	1.7
Market-value capital (MVP)	(12.7)	(17.9)	(14.4)	(8.3)	(2.7)	1.5	2.3	0.3	1.7

NOTE: GAAP capital consists of permanent, preferred, and common stock and retained earnings. TAP capital equals GAAP capital minus goodwill and other intangibles. RAP capital essentially equals GAAP capital plus deferred loan losses, appraised equity capital, subordinated debentures, mutual capital certificates, income capital certificates, net worth certificates, and regulatory forbearances such as the amortization of goodwill over periods longer than those prescribed by GAAP and the inclusion of FSLIC assistance in a merger accounted for under the purchase method. MVP capital is obtained basically by marking-to-market the fixed-rate mortgage portfolio.

SOURCE: Federal Home Loan Bank Board.

more rapidly than assets, big and prolonged increases in interest rates can clearly devastate savings and loan institutions. Thus, another cause of the current savings and loan misfortunes is unexpectedly high and volatile interest rates.

Deterioration in Asset Quality. Whereas the problem in the early 1980s was related mainly to interest rates, the problem in later years was related mainly to asset quality. Unlike interest rates, which simultaneously affect savings and loans nationwide, the quality of assets is determined primarily by local and regional factors that do not always move in tandem with national factors. In this regard, savings and loans in Texas, which was hard hit by sharply falling energy prices in the 1980s, accounted for the largest share of the total resolution costs during the decade. Comparing net nonoperating income for savings and loans in that state with net nonoperating income for all savings and loans, we find that net nonoperating losses for savings and loans in both Texas and the United States track one another quite closely from 1985 onward. As a result, total industry losses became increasingly concentrated in Texas after 1984, and most of the losses were due to asset write-downs and additions to loan loss reserves. The plunging oil prices and real estate values clearly contributed to the sharp deterioration in asset quality at Texas savings and loans. Thus, regional economic factors leading to deterioration in asset quality also caused problems for the savings and loans.

Federal and State Deregulation. As we know, savings and loans have been heavily regulated for years. Such regulation undoubtedly generated monopoly rents, enhancing the value of the savings and loan charter. But the savings and loans, with their institutional rigidity were thus vulnerable to changing market forces, since they could not adapt to technological developments dramatically affecting the methods and cost of producing and monitoring information. Unlike less regulated financial service firms, this inability to adapt drove the industry into deep insolvency in the late 1970s and early 1980s.

Congress enacted legislation in the early 1980s in response to the plight of the savings and loan industry. As appendix B shows, this legislation gave federally chartered institutions new and expanded powers. State authorities generally granted similar powers to state-chartered savings and loans, and even broader powers in some notable instances, sometimes years earlier. Under

40

its own authority, moreover, the federal regulator of savings and loans—the FHLBB until October 9, 1989, and the Office of Thrift Supervision thereafter—is free to vary the regulatory treatment of institutions with respect to certain activities. Appendix C shows the way in which this regulatory authority was used initially to loosen the regulatory grip on the practices and activities of savings and loans in the early 1980s and then to tighten it somewhat in the mid-1980s.

Although the deregulation during the early 1980s came after the industry was in serious trouble, it nonetheless increased competition among savings and loan institutions and other financial service firms throughout the remainder of the 1980s. As a result, some institutions failed. Still others, though, were undoubtably able to compete more effectively and thereby survived. To the extent that the casualties of the deregulation were inefficient savings and loans, deregulation per se was not bad. The fact that the timing was bad, causing an uneven and inappropriate expansion of powers granted to savings and loans, is not a criticism of deregulation. Furthermore, to the extent that deregulation provided inadequately capitalized institutions greater freedom to adopt go-for-broke strategies, the real culprit is delay in reorganizing or closing troubled institutions, not deregulation.

In any event, even though it may only have worsened the problem, deregulation nonetheless contributed to the difficulties facing the savings and loans. Not unexpectedly, deregulation led to skirmishes among some federal and state authorities as each accused the other of responsibility for the debacle. According to table 3–5 a large portion of the estimated present-value cost of resolving failed savings and loans from 1980 through 1988 was associated with state-chartered institutions. A closer examination of the data, however, reveals that an even larger portion of the cost is associated with stock-type savings and loans. In fact, the experience of the stock-type savings and loans in the 1980s was not an isolated incident in our nation's financial history. For, as Thomas Marvell pointed out more than twenty years ago in describing a situation with remarkable parallels,

> Although the 1960–65 expansion was beneficial in a way because it helped pull the country out of an economic recession and supplied a great deal of new mortgage money, many stock S&L's got into trouble by contin-

TABLE 3-5

SAVINGS AND LOANS' FAILURES AND RESOLUTION COSTS, BY CHARTER AND OWNERSHIP TYPE AND TOTAL ASSETS, 1980–1988

	Quarter before GAAP Insolvency				Quarter before Resolution			
	State charter		Federal charter		State charter		Federal charter	
	Stock	Mutual	Stock	Mutual	Stock	Mutual	Stock	Mutual
1980								
Number of institutions	3	4	0	4	3	4	0	4
Total assets	399	179	0	769	783	180	0	769
Estimated cost of resolution	18	17	0	131	18	17	0	131
1981								
Number of institutions	6	3	0	19	6	3	4	15
Total assets	513	1,979	0	8,955	513	1,979	1,196	7,741
Estimated cost of resolution	89	113	0	557	89	113	20	537
1982								
Number of institutions	12	8	0	43	11	8	2	42
Total assets	2,948	900	0	9,343	2,791	884	168	9,293
Estimated cost of resolution	263	40	0	500	246	40	17	500
1983								
Number of institutions	9	10	1	16	8	10	2	16
Total assets	928	1,560	45	2,081	814	1,565	140	2,057
Estimated cost of resolution	79	112	2	82	78	112	3	82

1984								
Number of institutions	10	3	1	8	8	2	3	9
Total assets	1,387	152	27	3,382	1,367	143	409	3,137
Estimated cost of resolution	565	8	7	163	528	7	44	164
1985								
Number of institutions	10	2	2	17	9	2	3	17
Total assets	2,144	159	698	3,818	1,616	153	890	3,772
Estimated cost of resolution	445	10	146	422	427	10	163	421
1986								
Number of institutions	20	4	4	18	18	3	5	20
Total assets	5,252	741	2,111	4,875	4,931	535	2,035	4,764
Estimated cost of resolution	1,411	128	821	705	1,394	128	838	705
1987								
Number of institutions	17	7	8	15	12	6	7	22
Total assets	4,291	3,815	4,607	2,809	1,050	2,399	812	6,289
Estimated cost of resolution	1,935	507	710	551	504	405	230	2,565
1988								
Number of institutions	98	17	22	68	75	13	18	99
Total assets	83,783	3,298	10,313	22,798	63,892	2,230	8,362	28,290
Estimated cost of resolution	22,686	597	2,665	4,954	18,706	546	2,121	9,492

NOTE: The estimated cost of resolution is in present-value terms for each year. The cost estimates and total assets are in millions of dollars.

SOURCE: Federal Home Loan Bank Board.

uing to expand even though there was considerable overbuilding of homes in their communities. The growth of stock S&L's was achieved by means that the FHLBB generally does not favor—aggressive advertising and the use of brokers. Also, a great deal of the funds acquired were used to make large risky loans for housing projects, which produced very high interest rates but tended to default frequently. A large percentage of the problem cases are stock S&L's—much larger than their share of the total industry—and they accounted for all five of the recent FSLIC insurance payouts (Marvell 1969, 245–46).

Fraudulent Practices. Savings and loan institutions can fail through fraud and insider abuse on the part of management or owners. Although quite difficult to detect beforehand, they can clearly be a source of trouble. Indeed, fraudulent activities have been found in roughly half the savings and loans resolved in 1988 (see Barth, April 1990). Furthermore, the Resolution Trust Corporation has found fraudulent activities in over half the insolvent savings and loans that came under its control within its first year of operation. Nevertheless, Barth, Bartholomew, and Labich (1989) estimate that fraud accounts for only about 10 percent of the resolution costs, and Ely (1990) estimates an even smaller figure of 3 percent. According to a senior official of the Office of Thrift Supervision, however, "Fraud losses are more in the 25 percent range" (Black, April 1990, 51). This same official observes that "with no money of their own at risk, the incentive to . . . engage in fraud proved compelling for many insiders" (Black, April 1989, 27). Fraud, then, is likely to flourish if regulation and supervision are lax. Regardless of the exact figure, Timothy Ryan, director of the Office of Thrift Supervision, is reported to have

> agreed that fraud probably was responsible for only a small percentage of the number of failed thrifts. He said that the media and politicians may have convinced many taxpayers that fraud was the main reason for the problem "because it was the easiest thing to focus on and understand" (King, *Atlanta Constitution* 1990, F–3).

Nonetheless, fraudulent practices, not to mention simple mismanagement, have played a part in the savings and loan debacle.

44

Increased Competition in the Financial Services Industry. Substantial improvements in informational technology, rapid growth in mortgage loan securitization, and greater competition among financial service firms in the 1970s and 1980s significantly narrowed the net interest margins for savings and loans. As a result, only the lowest-cost providers of services and products have been able to remain relatively profitable. Table 3–6 shows that insured depository institutions collectively experienced a substantially declining share of the assets of all financial service firms as new services and products came into existence and generated expanding opportunities for noninsured and less regulated firms in the 1980s. Because this increased competition contributed to the disappearance of many savings and loans, it is therefore another cause of the problems.

Tax Law Changes. The Tax Reform Act of 1986 reduced the depreciation benefits from investing in commercial and residential property, limited the offsetting losses on passive investments that affect limited partnership syndications, and eliminated the favorable capital gains treatment. The changes in tax laws adversely affected real estate values, thereby weakening the financial condition of savings and loan institutions. Tax law changes, then, also contributed to the industry's strains.

Moral Hazard. Federal deposit insurance was established in response to the widespread failure of financial institutions during the Great Depression. The main rationale for such insurance is that without it depositors might attempt to withdraw their funds whenever a commercial bank or savings and loan was believed to be insolvent. In a world of uncertainty, the withdrawals might not be restricted to insolvent institutions but instead spread to solvent ones. Although the Federal Reserve System as the lender-of-last-resort has the responsibility of lending to illiquid but solvent institutions, it must have sufficient information to distinguish between solvent and insolvent institutions (see Barth and Keleher 1984; and Kaufman, May 18–19, 1990, for a discussion of the role of the lender-of-last-resort when a federal deposit insurance system exists). The benefit of federal deposit insurance is that, if successful, it resolves this informational problem by assuring depositors that their funds are so safe that they need not engage in a run on depository institutions. This benefit comes at a cost, however. So long as depositors believe their funds are totally se-

TABLE 3–6: PERCENTAGE OF TOTAL U.S. FINANCIAL ASSETS HELD BY FINANCIAL SERVICE FIRMS, 1980–1988

	1980	1981	1982	1983	1984	1985	1986	1987	1988
Depository Institutions									
Commercial banks	36.8	36.3	35.2	34.2	34.0	33.1	31.9	31.2	30.4
U.S.-chartered	31.4	30.6	29.9	29.1	28.9	27.9	26.5	25.5	24.7
Foreign offices in U.S.	2.5	2.8	2.3	2.0	2.0	2.1	2.3	2.6	2.7
Domestic affiliates	2.6	2.6	2.7	2.8	3.0	3.1	3.0	3.0	2.9
Banks in U.S. possessions	0.3	0.3	0.3	0.2	0.1	0.1	0.1	0.1	0.1
Savings and loans	15.2	14.6	14.2	14.9	15.7	14.8	13.9	14.1	14.1
Mutual savings banks	4.3	3.9	3.5	3.5	3.3	3.1	2.9	3.0	2.9
Credit unions	1.7	1.6	1.7	1.8	1.8	1.9	2.0	2.1	2.0
Contractual Intermediaries									
Life insurance companies	11.5	11.4	11.5	11.5	11.1	11.1	11.0	11.3	11.5
Other insurance companies	4.3	4.2	4.1	4.1	3.9	4.0	4.2	4.4	4.5
Private pension funds	11.6	10.9	11.7	12.4	11.5	11.9	11.5	11.4	11.8
State and local government retirement funds	4.9	5.0	5.3	5.7	5.7	5.7	5.7	5.8	6.3
Others									
Finance companies	5.0	5.1	4.8	4.8	4.8	4.9	5.0	5.1	5.1
Mutual funds	1.5	1.3	1.6	2.0	2.2	3.4	5.1	5.2	4.9
Security brokers and dealers	1.1	1.4	1.7	1.7	1.9	2.2	2.3	1.6	1.5
Money market mutual funds	1.9	4.2	4.5	3.3	3.7	3.4	3.6	3.6	3.5
REITS	0.1	0.1	0.1	0.1	0.1	0.1	0.1	0.1	0.1
SCO issuers	0.0	0.0	0.0	0.1	0.2	0.4	0.8	1.2	1.4
Total assets ($ billions)	4,032	4,455	4,916	5,503	6,232	7,141	8,185	8,840	9,667

SOURCE: Flow of Funds Accounts, Board of Governors of the Federal Reserve System.

cure, they have no incentive to impose discipline on the way the institutions use those funds. An institution can therefore invest federally insured deposits in riskier activities than would otherwise be possible. The government's role is to contain this "moral hazard" problem by mimicking the private market (that is, doing what depositors at risk would do). To the extent that the regulator does not properly control the risk-taking behavior of institutions, more failures and greater failure costs are likely than would be possible without deposit insurance (see Buser, Chen, and Kane 1981). More important, the value of insurance to an institution, and hence its proclivity toward risk-taking behavior, varies inversely with the amount of the owner-contributed equity capital at risk (see Keeley and Furlong 1989). No matter what factors initially cause savings and loans to become inadequately capitalized, then, deposit insurance will permit such institutions to retain access to funds by offering high rates and thus continue operating in a go-for-broke manner. The rule by which the regulator reorganizes or closes troubled institutions is crucial to preventing institutions from gambling for resurrection with federally insured deposits. Without timely reorganization or closure when owner-contributed equity capital has been depleted, a troubled institution may become an even greater problem. In this sense, delay itself is costly to the insurer. In sum, the structure of the federal deposit insurance system is yet another cause of the debacle.

Sorting through the Evidence for a Unifying Cause

According to the unwritten law of long tradition, a leading function of the bank supervisor was to ascertain the extent of equity in banks by determining their liabilities and appraising their assets. Whenever the liabilities of a bank exceeded the appraised value of the assets or whenever capital was seriously impaired, it was his duty to take action to remedy this situation. If stockholders' contributions or sales of stock did not yield sufficient new money, he brought pressure to achieve a reorganization or a merger or, failing in this, urged the board of directors to close the bank. This traditional policy was defended upon the grounds that without it . . . de-

47

positors would suffer much greater losses than if the bank had been closed at once.

Supervisors had also commonly concerned themselves with the volume of bank capital, even though it was not technically impaired, since capital was considered a cushion against asset depreciation. Accordingly, in cases of inadequacy they took steps to secure its increase (Jones 1940, 183–84).

All the factors that have been identified combined to cause the savings and loan disaster of the 1980s. Yet, it is important to focus on the specific role played by the structure of the federal deposit insurance system. As already noted, depositor discipline is absent for those with federal insurance, which was $100,000 per account throughout the 1980s, having been raised by Congress from $40,000 per account in 1980. The government therefore has the responsibility to impose discipline on savings and loan institutions. But did this indeed happen? An assessment of available evidence indicates that federal deposit insurance itself is the unifying cause of the savings and loans' misfortunes.

Capital Required at Savings and Loans

Figure 3–1 presents information on the three major alternative accounting measures of capital expressed as a percentage of assets for all savings and loans. Regardless of the measure used, capital declined precipitously during the early 1980s. The measure of capital based on regulatory accounting practices (RAP) declined the least because it is significantly broader than the capital measure based upon generally accepted accounting principles (GAAP). The strictest or most conservative accounting measure (TAP)—for tangible accounting principles—of capital deducts goodwill and other intangibles from GAAP capital. Despite the decline in all three measures and the resulting increase in the FSLIC's risk exposure, the capital requirements were reduced. In 1980, the Depository Institutions Deregulation and Monetary Control Act removed the 5 percent minimum statutory capital requirement then in effect. Instead, the FHLBB was mandated to set the regulatory requirement simply within the statutory range of 3 to 6 percent. The FHLBB responded by lowering the regulatory requirement to 4 from 5 percent in November 1980.

FIGURE 3–1
CAPITAL-TO-ASSET RATIOS FOR SAVINGS AND LOANS, 1940–1989

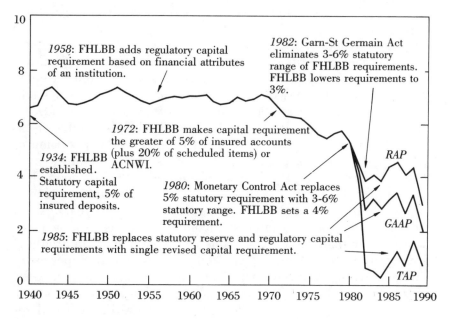

SOURCE: Barth (1990).

The regulatory requirement was lowered still further to 3 percent in January 1982. Then later in 1982, the Garn-St Germain Depository Institutions Act deleted the 3 to 6 percent statutory capital requirement, with the mandate that the FHLBB simply require "adequate" capital. In addition to lowering the capital requirements, the FHLBB broadened the items counting as RAP capital beyond those permitted under GAAP. In particular, in September 1981 savings and loans could defer and amortize gains and losses on the sale of mortgage loans, mortgage-related securities, and debt securities. (At the time, of course, they were experiencing only losses on such sales.) GAAP, in contrast, requires the immediate recognition of gains and losses. In November 1982 savings and loans were also permitted to include in RAP capital "appraised equity capital," which is the difference between the book value and the market value of the office, land, buildings, and improvements owned by the institution or any of its subsidiaries. All these as well as other changes in the regulatory capital requirements during the 1980s are presented in ap-

49

pendix D. Such regulatory accounting changes clearly moderated the decline in RAP capital during the early 1980s.

Another important accounting issue concerns the regulatory treatment of goodwill and its effect on income and capital for savings and loans. Figure 3–1 clearly shows that TAP capital declined the most rapidly in the early 1980s. GAAP capital did not decline similarly because it includes goodwill and an enormous amount of goodwill was put onto the books of savings and loans during the early 1980s, particularly as a result of all the supervisory mergers arranged by the FHLBB (see table 3–2). When savings and loans were merged under the supervision of the FHLBB, the assets of the troubled institutions were written down to their market value based on the purchase method of accounting. This write-down or discount was then amortized over the remaining life of the assets, usually five to ten years, as an upward adjustment to interest income. If the acquisition price was greater than the market value of the capital of the troubled savings and loan, which was certainly the case for the supervisory mergers arranged in the early 1980s, the difference was recorded as goodwill and amortized as an expense for a period up to forty years beginning in July 1982—before then the FHLBB had required the amortization of goodwill over no more than ten years. Since the amortization period of the discount was much shorter than the amortization period of the goodwill, the resulting increase in interest income exceeded the increase in expenses. The general effect of the supervisory mergers was, therefore, to increase significantly reported net income and regulatory capital for a long time after the merger (see Black, Spring 1990). In June 1982, goodwill amounted to $7.9 billion, but by December 1983 it had increased to $30.0 billion and represented more than 90 percent of total RAP capital.

Three other points with respect to capital should be mentioned. First, the regulatory capital requirements were calculated at the end of each year before 1986. Second, from August 1982 to April 1985, 100 percent of regulatory capital could consist of subordinated debt so long as its remaining term-to-maturity exceeded one year. Third, until the regulatory capital requirements were completely restructured in January 1985, the calculation of the requirement permitted the use of five-year averaging (a technique that took the average of the insured deposits on the annual closing date and on one or more of the four immediately preceding annual closing dates) and twenty-year phase-in techniques (which provided for the gradual buildup, by a specified annual percentage, to a stated capital requirement over a twenty-year period).

All these changes in the capital requirements reduced the amount of owner-contributed equity capital that had to be injected into savings and loans. The leverage potential, in other words, was dramatically expanded, despite the common knowledge that, as was even pointed out at the time federal deposit insurance was established, "the possibility of losing owners' capital is, without doubt, the strongest force in operation to prevent unsound banking" (Taggart and Jennings 1934, 514–15). Worse yet, the capital requirement was reduced at a time when information revealing the extent of the problems in the industry was available. In July 1981, for example, the *Report of the Task Force on Savings and Loan Portfolio Profitability* stated that the industry's net worth "was overstated by $152.3 billion, on market value versus book value basis, at the end of 1980" (p. 2). More important, as the chairman of the FHLBB in the early 1980s stated, "By 1982, the real capital positions of all thrift institutions had been completely eroded, and virtually all thrift institutions had large negative net worths when their assets and liabilities were valued at actual market rates" (Pratt 1988, 4). Yet, inadequately capitalized institutions have every incentive to engage in high-risk activities or to gamble for resurrection. It is the "heads I win, tails the federal insurer loses" scenario at work. By not being forced to reorganize or close, inadequately capitalized savings and loans were given time to pursue the end-game or go-for-broke strategies and were completely funded with federally insured deposits. To quote from Edward Kane, one of the very first to write about these issues, "In an economic environment in which deposit institutions are highly levered and entering new businesses every day and in which interest rates are highly volatile, systematically mispricing deposit-insurance guarantees encourages deposit-institution managers to position their firms on the edge of financial disaster" (Kane 1986, 100). The moral hazard problem was simply not contained in the savings and loan industry during the 1980s, as indicated by evidence presented in Barth, Bartholomew, and Labich (1989) and Brewer (1990). The role of the insurer is to recognize and acknowledge losses and then to contain and minimize them through appropriate action, not simply to paper over the losses in the hope they will go away over time. Admittedly,

TABLE 3–7
FEDERAL HOME LOAN BANK BOARD ENFORCEMENT ACTIONS, 1980–1988

Calendar Year	Cease-and-Desist Orders	Number of Individuals Removed and/or Prohibited	Supervisory Agreements	Consent Merger Resolutions and Agreements	Number of Investigations Completed by Office of Enforcement	
					Formal	Informal
1980	3	1	1	6	6	10
1981	8	2	0	33	8	6
1982	13	6	5	49	10	10
1983	17	21	39	22	17	15
1984	13	22	116	38	24	20
1985	28	22	233	65	30	30
1986	58	48	214	130	30	25
1987	25	44	106	102	40	28
1988	26	47	107	98	35	30

SOURCE: Federal Home Loan Bank Board.

as the data in table 3–7 indicate, the FHLBB did implement enforcement actions against savings and loans during the 1980s. Given what was known about the seriousness of the problem and the way in which the industry grew in size throughout the 1980s, however, one must question whether these actions were either sufficiently numerous or sufficiently stringent. In any event, the appropriate action for dealing with inadequately capitalized institutions, of course, requires *both* adequate funds *and* good personnel to work out the problems to protect the taxpayers as much as possible.

Low Regulatory Capital Requirements and Stock Ownership

The form of ownership for savings and loans is important because, as indicated earlier (see table 3–5), stock-type institutions accounted for 77 percent of the total estimated present-value resolution costs from 1980 through 1988. Examining this issue more closely, one finds that in the fall of 1982 the Garn-St Germain Depository Institutions Act authorized the FHLBB to charter federal savings and loans in either mutual or stock form. A federal institution could therefore be authorized to convert from mutual to stock, or a *de novo* federal institution could be authorized to operate in stock form. State-chartered institutions in many states were already able to request authorization to operate in either mutual or stock form. The FHLBB, in April 1982, moreover, had eliminated all restrictions relating to: (1) the minimum number of stockholders (formerly 400 in counties with a population greater than 100,000); and (2) the aggregate ownership of stock by individuals (formerly not more than 10 percent of the total stock) and families or businesses (formerly not more than 25 percent of the total stock).

The FHLBB also eliminated the requirement that 75 percent of the stockholders must reside or do business in the market area of a savings and loan. This regulatory change meant that one person or business firm could become the sole stockholder of a stock-type institution. Given the general relaxation of the regulatory capital requirements, both the reduction in the required percentages and the additional items that could be counted as regulatory capital, there was effectively only a minimal amount of contributed equity capital that owners were required to inject into a stock-type institution. In the case of a *de novo* stock-type institution, the leverage ratio was enormous, and the ability to pay out dividends meant that the return on owner-contributed equity capital could be astronomical.

This setting was particularly conducive to the pursuit of high-risk investment strategies funded with federally insured deposits. Risky investment was made all the easier when the powers for savings and loans were expanded by federal legislation in the early 1980s and by legislation in such states as California, Florida, and Texas, which granted state-chartered institutions powers beyond those granted to federally chartered institutions. In California, for example, state-chartered institutions were permitted—effective January 1, 1983—to invest in real estate for development and in service corporations without any percentage of asset limitations. To establish a *de novo* stock-type institution to engage in these activities, the FHLBB required a minimum of $2.0 million in initial capital stock for institutions locating in counties with a population greater than 100,000. Based on the 3 percent capital requirement for state-chartered institutions in California, a new stock-type institution had the potential to leverage the $2.0 million in owner-contributed equity capital to $66.7 million in assets by the end of the first year in operation. Based on the twenty-year phase-in techniques (which required an institution to increase its capital in 0.15 percent multiples from 0.15 percent of insured deposits at the end of the first year in operation to 3 percent at the end of twenty years) for federally chartered institutions, a new stock-type institution could leverage the $2.0 million in owner-contributed equity capital to $1.3 billion in assets by the end of the first year in operation. Such phenomenal growth could be funded entirely by federally insured deposits, including brokered deposits. Not surprisingly, the number of applications for state charters in California increased to ninety-nine in the first six months of 1983, up from forty-three in all of 1982, and up from four in 1981. More generally, table 3–8 shows the growth in both the number and the assets of federally and state-chartered stock-type institutions as compared with mutual-type savings and loans over the period 1979 to 1988 in California, Florida, and Texas, as well as nationwide. The total increase in assets was greatest at stock-type savings and loans, particularly in the two years subsequent to all the regulatory developments in 1982 that loosened the constraints on these types of institutions. Table 3–9, more-

TABLE 3–8
CHARTER AND OWNERSHIP OF SAVINGS AND LOANS IN CALIFORNIA, FLORIDA, TEXAS, AND THE UNITED STATES, 1979–1988
(millions of dollars)

	Federal						State					
	Mutual			Stock			Mutual			Stock		
	Number	Assets	Growth (%)	Number	Assets	Growth (%)	Number	Assets	Growth (%)	Number	Assets	Growth (%)
California												
1979	69	35,818		3	168		8	1,045		99	70,316	
1980	65	36,112	1	4	202	20	8	1,105	6	118	80,748	15
1981	54	41,349	15	13	33,387	16,428	5	805	−27	115	52,282	−35
1982	44	50,882	23	20	70,681	112	2	268	−67	105	29,166	−44
1983	37	25,579	−50	22	109,150	54	3	2,658	891	119	55,841	91
1984	25	13,186	−48	28	124,397	14	5	10,988	314	142	102,209	83
1985	33	21,066	60	31	139,603	12	5	11,626	6	150	100,614	−2
1986	23	11,873	−44	43	165,498	19	4	3,857	−87	146	127,480	27
1987	28	11,188	−8	41	190,703	15	3	1,685	−58	134	142,147	12
1988	18	5,762	−48	48	269,799	41	3	1,688	0	124	117,567	−17
Florida												
1979	108	37,744		3	1,911		5	3,168		6	2,111	
1980	100	38,899	3	7	3,570	87	6	3,834	21	13	3,911	85

(Table 3–8 continues)

TABLE 3–8 (continued)

| | Federal | | | | | | | | State | | | | | | | |
| | Mutual | | | Stock | | | Mutual | | | Stock | | | | | | |
	Number	Assets	Growth (%)	Number	Assets	Growth (%)	Number	Assets	Growth (%)	Number	Assets	Growth (%)
1981	92	40,939	5	11	7,050	97	4	2,938	−23	21	4,579	17
1982	75	37,969	−7	10	7,738	10	4	3,119	6	24	4,477	−2
1983	74	44,788	18	8	6,397	−17	4	3,607	16	28	7,505	68
1984	55	29,942	−33	27	26,765	318	1	211	−94	40	18,407	145
1985	52	28,340	−5	38	29,024	8	2	993	371	51	22,680	23
1986	49	28,489	1	41	26,214	−10	1	854	−14	58	27,247	20
1987	47	25,022	−12	43	26,175	0	1	882	3	57	27,950	3
1988	38	22,059	−12	53	33,540	28	1	973	10	52	31,961	14
Texas												
1979	67	7,288		2	284		34	3,375		207	19,325	
1980	67	7,955	9	1	91	−68	35	3,722	10	215	22,105	14
1981	62	8,221	3	4	345	279	31	3,900	5	210	24,694	12

1982	51	8,706	6	3	127	−63	28	4,153	6	198	29,020	18
1983	51	10,034	15	5	361	184	26	4,509	9	186	41,074	42
1984	40	7,165	−29	18	6,170	1,609	21	5,250	16	188	58,768	43
1985	36	6,660	−7	22	6,212	1	17	4,431	−16	198	74,281	26
1986	41	9,582	44	25	5,041	−19	16	4,089	−8	199	77,876	5
1987	43	10,638	11	25	6,608	31	15	4,385	7	196	77,676	0
1988	28	16,488	55	29	36,733	456	11	3,819	−13	136	53,522	−31

United States

1979	1,964	308,580		24	6,530		1,333	106,286		717	132,955	15
1980	1,945	327,772	6	39	11,799	81	1,266	111,751	5	743	152,448	−16
1981	1,818	345,944	6	79	55,165	368	1,147	110,144	−1	707	128,554	−16
1982	1,588	380,629	10	104	98,482	79	959	98,214	−11	636	108,214	37
1983	1,550	411,515	8	127	148,775	51	869	103,753	6	600	148,464	61
1984	1,398	354,657	−14	291	271,670	83	804	111,713	8	643	239,411	14
1985	1,344	354,843	0	377	328,605	21	815	112,335	1	710	272,478	16
1986	1,264	341,082	−4	480	404,686	23	767	101,116	−10	709	314,718	9
1987	1,193	385,815	−16	575	527,409	30	685	92,904	−8	694	342,738	−12
1988	1,043	269,214	−6	677	691,844	31	621	87,889	−5	608	300,074	

SOURCE: Federal Home Loan Bank Board.

57

TABLE 3-9

Portfolio Composition of Savings and Loans in Selected States and the United States, 1980–1988

	Capital-to-Asset Ratio, 12/80					Capital-to-Asset Ratio, 12/81					Capital-to-Asset Ratio, 12/82				
	S&Ls resolved	<0%	0%–3%	>3%	All	S&Ls resolved	<0%	0%–3%	>3%	All	S&Ls resolved	<0%	0%–3%	>3%	All
Texas															
Traditional ratio	NA	51.2	68.9	75.4	74.6	41.8	66.1	73.3	76.5	75.5	57.6	67.1	67.9	71.7	70.0
Risky ratio	NA	2.1	4.9	2.4	2.5	0.0	5.1	2.9	2.6	2.7	5.7	4.1	6.6	4.6	5.0
Number of institutions	0	7	19	292	318	1	8	66	233	307	8	43	71	166	280
California															
Traditional ratio	NA	63.1	76.3	80.6	80.3	NA	75.8	74.8	79.0	78.3	77.9	70.4	72.1	71.5	71.5
Risky ratio	NA	0.0	1.2	1.8	1.8	NA	2.1	3.9	2.2	2.5	0.0	4.2	3.7	3.0	3.3
Number of institutions	0	2	9	184	195	0	6	28	153	187	2	15	37	119	171
Florida															
Traditional ratio	76.0	30.8	83.1	83.8	82.8	82.6	86.0	81.0	77.6	78.9	82.3	75.4	77.6	68.9	73.1
Risky ratio	0.8	0.0	1.0	1.4	1.3	1.3	0.7	1.6	1.8	1.7	1.0	2.2	2.0	3.2	2.6
Number of institutions	1	2	19	105	126	3	3	43	82	128	2	21	39	53	113
Illinois															
Traditional ratio	82.2	NA	79.1	83.4	82.9	80.2	73.0	80.1	82.0	81.2	79.1	71.8	77.5	80.4	78.3
Risky ratio	3.8	NA	2.4	1.5	1.6	6.3	3.7	1.9	1.2	1.5	3.1	2.0	1.5	1.1	1.4

	Capital-to-Asset Ratio, 12/83					Capital-to-Asset Ratio, 12/84					Capital-to-Asset Ratio, 12/85				
	S&Ls resolved	<0%	0%–3%	>3%	All	S&Ls resolved	<0%	0%–3%	>3%	All	S&Ls resolved	<0%	0%–3%	>3%	All
Number of institutions	2	0	42	328	370	5	11	97	231	339	13	40	89	163	292
United States															
Traditional ratio	80.7	63.4	76.6	82.0	81.4	79.9	71.8	77.4	80.6	79.8	77.7	69.4	74.9	77.8	76.1
Risky ratio	1.8	0.9	1.5	1.1	1.2	2.1	2.1	1.7	1.2	1.3	2.0	2.4	2.0	1.4	1.7
Number of institutions	11	43	293	3,657	3,993	28	112	702	2,937	3,751	63	389	846	2,052	3,287
Texas															
Traditional ratio	51.9	60.6	65.9	66.1	64.8	40.0	51.1	54.7	60.0	55.7	2.8	42.6	47.7	54.2	48.5
Risky ratio	1.2	8.2	10.5	8.2	8.8	24.6	12.9	15.3	10.9	12.8	29.7	17.9	19.4	13.8	16.8
Number of institutions	1	61	71	136	268	2	85	76	106	267	1	90	80	103	273
California															
Traditional ratio	NA	72.2	71.2	71.8	71.7	11.4	60.7	64.2	61.8	62.6	0.1	48.3	61.1	64.0	60.5
Risky ratio	NA	4.1	5.3	6.3	5.8	27.3	7.1	6.9	6.3	6.7	6.4	14.3	8.4	5.5	7.8
Number of institutions	0	19	54	108	181	1	29	81	90	200	1	38	59	122	219
Florida															
Traditional ratio	NA	68.8	73.3	69.6	70.6	NA	63.1	60.0	61.2	61.3	14.7	56.5	63.6	62.3	61.4
Risky ratio	NA	3.4	2.4	4.8	3.8	NA	4.4	5.8	6.0	5.6	1.6	8.0	6.5	6.0	6.6

(Table 3–9 continues)

TABLE 3-9 (continued)

	Capital-to-Asset Ratio, 12/80					Capital-to-Asset Ratio, 12/81					Capital-to-Asset Ratio, 12/82				
	S&Ls resolved	<0%	0%–3%	>3%	All	S&Ls resolved	<0%	0%–3%	>3%	All	S&Ls resolved	<0%	0%–3%	>3%	All
Number of institutions	0	25	34	55	114	0	29	40	54	123	1	30	38	76	144
Illinois															
Traditional ratio	55.9	70.5	75.7	78.0	75.7	9.7	64.6	71.2	75.3	70.8	36.8	59.9	68.6	71.0	66.8
Risky ratio	11.6	2.3	1.3	0.9	1.4	13.9	1.9	2.0	0.8	1.4	2.6	2.4	1.4	0.9	1.5
Number of institutions	2	61	81	134	276	1	90	66	117	273	1	91	50	128	269
United States															
Traditional ratio	67.8	67.6	72.6	75.7	73.6	19.4	61.9	67.0	72.4	68.6	16.2	57.0	65.0	69.9	66.1
Risky ratio	2.0	3.1	2.7	2.2	2.5	7.7	4.1	4.0	2.4	3.2	3.9	57.3	5.2	2.8	3.9
Number of institutions	36	515	876	1,755	3,146	22	713	874	1,660	3,247	31	714	739	1,888	3,341

	Capital-to-Asset Ratio, 12/86					Capital-to-Asset Ratio, 12/87					Capital-to-Asset Ratio, 12/88				
	S&Ls resolved	<0%	0%–3%	>3%	All	S&Ls resolved	<0%	0%–3%	>3%	All	S&Ls resolved	<0%	0%–3%	>3%	All
Texas															
Traditional ratio	4.9	36.0	49.0	54.2	45.2	8.5	32.9	50.6	56.6	42.7	28.1	34.6	47.2	57.8	44.5
Risky ratio	14.4	18.0	17.0	11.3	15.5	19.5	13.4	13.1	8.0	11.8	11.3	10.4	9.7	6.2	8.9

Number of institutions	2	122	98	281	4	152	48	79	279	81	97	44	63	204
California														
Traditional ratio	14.3	46.1	65.7	61.3	19.9	44.9	67.4	69.3	64.4	34.7	52.2	65.3	71.5	67.6
Risky ratio	11.6	9.0	4.6	5.8	8.1	6.7	4.3	4.5	4.9	7.5	3.3	4.0	4.8	4.4
Number of institutions	8	40	140	216	5	39	29	138	206	18	24	47	122	193
Florida														
Traditional ratio	8.9	52.6	65.7	62.3	NA	52.8	62.2	70.0	65.3	44.8	54.8	63.4	71.3	66.9
Risky ratio	35.5	7.0	5.1	5.4	NA	6.1	4.3	4.5	4.8	8.6	4.3	4.3	5.4	5.0
Number of institutions	2	31	92	150	0	32	20	97	149	7	27	25	93	145
Illinois														
Traditional ratio	15.7	57.8	69.4	65.0	4.7	60.9	67.8	72.2	68.3	57.3	62.5	66.5	72.9	69.4
Risky ratio	4.6	2.2	1.5	1.7	1.5	1.6	1.0	1.2	1.3	1.9	1.8	1.3	2.1	1.9
Number of institutions	1	82	139	267	3	75	44	145	264	15	58	38	151	247
United States														
Traditional ratio	15.4	51.8	68.8	64.2	13.0	50.1	64.7	71.7	66.1	43.3	52.3	64.3	72.7	68.0
Risky ratio	8.0	6.6	2.8	3.9	7.5	5.8	3.7	2.3	3.3	7.0	4.8	3.6	2.9	3.3
Number of institutions	46	680	2,022	3,289	47	677	475	2,060	3,212	205	506	450	2,060	3,016

NA = not applicable.

NOTES: All ratios in percentage points. Definition of ratios: traditional ratio equals 1–4 and >5 mortgages plus mortgage backed securities divided by total liabilities; risky ratio equals acquisition and development loans plus direct investment divided by total liabilities.
SOURCE: Federal Home Loan Bank Board.

61

over, presents information on the way in which the composition of portfolios changed over time when savings and loans are grouped by different capitalization levels. The data are consistent with the view that inadequately capitalized institutions increasingly shifted their portfolios toward high-risk activities over the period 1980 to 1986.

Delay in Reorganizing or Closing
Insolvent Savings and Loans

If an insolvent bank is taken over promptly and its affairs administered by competent men, the loss to depositors may be greatly minimized. Otherwise, the yield from assets may be small and expenses large. There is considerable evidence of delays, inefficiency and political influence (McCanan 1932, 170).

This observation applies equally well to the events that occurred in the savings and loan industry in the 1980s as to those in the commercial banking industry over a half-century ago. As table 3–10 shows, all the savings and loans that were resolved throughout the 1980s had *reported* their insolvency for years before finally being resolved. The 205 institutions resolved in 1988, for example, had reported being insolvent, on average, for forty months, or three and a half years. Some of these institutions had even been reporting insolvency for over ten years. Although an underestimate of the degree of market value insolvency, this book value measure was nevertheless an indicator of "true" insolvency (see Barth, Brumbaugh, and Sauerhaft 1986). Even in Texas, which accounted for the largest portion of the total estimated resolution costs in the 1980s, a large number of the resolved institutions had been reporting insolvency years before the major problems of asset quality surfaced. Besides the resolved institutions, 517 savings and loans were tangible-insolvent at year-end 1989. Even these particular institutions had been reporting their insolvency, on average, for forty-two consecutive months. Clearly, only with federal deposit insurance could institutions not only remain open for years but also continue to grow by offering relatively high rates on deposits, all the while publicly *reporting* their insolvency. The costliest resolutions in 1988, for instance, were offering an average of up to 100 basis points more on their deposits than other institutions in the year before resolution (see

62

TABLE 3-10

Comparison of Savings and Loan Institution Resolutions in the United States and Texas, 1980–1989

	Number of Resolutions		Total Assets of Resolutions ($ millions)		Estimated Present-Value Resolution Cost ($ millions)		Average Number of Months of TAP Insolvency	
	U.S.	Texas	U.S.	Texas	U.S.	Texas	U.S.	Texas
1980	11	0	1,458	0	167	0	5	0
1981	28	1	15,908	6	759	1	5	31
1982	63	8	17,662	1,031	806	78	8	11
1983	36	1	4,631	97	275	0	16	30
1984	22	2	5,080	348	743	164	23	16
1985	31	1	6,366	174	1,026	155	26	5
1986	46	2	12,455	1,080	3,065	493	31	14
1987	47	4	10,660	1,507	3,704	1,504	35	30
1988	205	81	101,242	35,978	31,790	19,491	42	38
1989	37	8	9,774	3,047	5,608	2,953	40	41

NOTE: Figures for 1989 may differ from previous years because of different methods of calculation by FSLIC and RTC. Resolution data for 1988 do not include eighteen "stabilizations" that at year-end 1988 had assets of $7.463 million and tangible net worth of negative $3.348 million, and an estimated present-value resolution cost of $6.838 million. Resolution data for 1989 do not include two RTC cases reportedly resolved without cost to the RTC.
SOURCE: Barth (April 1990).

Barth, Bartholomew, and Labich 1989). Such high rates not only adversely affect competing institutions but also almost always increase the losses that the government must bear. Furthermore, offering higher rates to retain deposits enables an inadequately capitalized institution to keep from selling assets at prices below book value, thereby avoiding the need to report losses and hence lower regulatory capital levels. In any event, had troubled savings and loans been reorganized or closed in a more timely and cost-effective manner, the cost of the savings and loan debacle would have been significantly lower. Indeed, as Dan Brumbaugh states: "As long as the insurer closes an institution before it is insolvent, the institution's risk-taking cannot affect insured depositors, and thus impose the social costs that deposit insurance was designed to avoid" (Brumbaugh 1988, 127).

Accurate Measures of Capital

Capital serves two functions. First, it protects the federal insurer, and hence the taxpayers, against declines in the value of assets relative to liabilities. Second, it imposes discipline by putting the owners' funds at risk. Yet the degree of protection afforded the insurer and the amount of discipline imposed depend on the amount of capital in an institution. It is therefore extremely important to measure capital as accurately as possible. As a former chairman of the FHLBB stated in the early 1980s, however,

> The management and accounting information now being generated within institutions and reported to the Federal Home Loan Bank Board and other supervisors is generally obsolete. Because historical generally accepted accounting principles (GAAP) fail to account for the real changes in the performance of financial institutions, it may lead to managerial behavior which seeks a certain historical cost accounting result but which actually damages both the institution, the insurance corporation and the regulator (Pratt 1983, 5).

As a possible solution to this problem, he suggested that "institutions should provide a better measurement of 'real' equity capital, using aspects of current value accounting, which will indicate the 'real' capital of an institution" (Pratt 1983, 5). The general

64

counsel of the FHLBB at the time stated that

> Over the last 18 months, the Board has continued to scrutinize the different forms of current market value booking to ensure that its policies accurately reflect relevant economic circumstances. In that respect, on November 4, 1982, the Board authorized inclusion within net worth of the market value appreciation of appraised equity capital. Likewise, Board staff is continuing to study the merits of an unprecedented proposed regulation to transform the historical cost accounting used by financial institutions to current market value accounting in order to measure more realistically the actual economic position of thrift institutions (Vartanian 1983, 11–12).

Indeed, the first chairman of the FDIC stated nearly sixty years ago "that a great many . . . bank statements in the past did not really show the true conditions of the banks." He added that "the old condensed statements gotten out by national banks and state banks for years . . . did not show the market value of their bonds or the reasonable value of their loans" (Crowley 1935, 97). Under the circumstances, is it any surprise that depositors would run on the depository institutions at the first sign of trouble without the protection of federal deposit insurance? At the time, moreover, depositors could use post offices, which were safe and secure places for their money, for, beginning in 1910, Congress authorized post offices to function as federally guaranteed savings banks. As a result, "From 1929 to 1934 the number of depositors rose from 417,000 to 2,563,000 and the level of funds deposited increased from $154 million to $1.2 billion" (Sorkin 1980, 9–10). It is unclear how many commercial banks or savings and loans may have experienced heavy withdrawals because of this service provided by the post offices.

The importance of an accurate measure of capital cannot be overstated. As has been recently pointed out, "Unless financial regulators begin to monitor and control leverage on the basis of market values, the question of asset deregulation is not fundamental. An insured institution can engage in risk-taking by leverage as well as by taking on asset risk" (Pyle 1985, 724). An accurate measure of capital is absolutely crucial if an inadequately capitalized institution is to be reorganized or closed in a timely and cost-effective manner (see Barth, Page, and Brumbaugh 1990, for an example of an approach to measuring owner-contributed equity capital for savings and loans). In this respect, one of the five grounds specified in the Home Owner's Loan Act of 1933 for the appointment of a conservator or receiver for a federally or state-chartered institution is insolvency. In enacting this legislation, however, Congress did not specify the particular valuation or accounting principles to be used by the FHLBB to determine solvency. Yet, throughout its existence, the FHLBB relied on a book valuation standard and regulatory accounting practices. Relying on such a self-imposed standard in the early 1980s, the FHLBB with a stroke of the regulatory pen was able to restore hundreds of savings and loans to "solvency." (As a historical aside, it should be noted that one institution challenged a receivership appointment by the FHLBB on the grounds that an insolvency determination must be based upon a market valuation rather than a book valuation standard.) As will be discussed in the next chapter, in 1989 Congress restricted the ability of the regulator of savings and loans to grant such capital forbearances in the future.

Four Savings and Loan Resolutions

Table 3–11 presents selected characteristics of four savings and loans that were resolved in 1988. These institutions had been reporting insolvency from thirty to seventy-five months before being resolved. The costliest resolution reported being insolvent for seventy-six months—that is, since 1982—before finally being resolved. During 1983–1985 all four savings and loans grew fairly rapidly, with one actually growing by more than 1,000 percent. The two costliest resolutions were closely held, stock-type institutions, having undergone changes in ownership control in the 1980s. The least costly resolution, unlike the others, was a mutual-type institution and displayed a portfolio revealing below industry-average involvement in the so-called high-risk investments. Although all three stock-type institutions relied more heavily on brokered deposits than all savings and loan institutions, the second most costly institution to resolve funded 35 percent of its assets with such deposits. In a study of commercial banks,

66

TABLE 3-11
FACTS ABOUT RESOLUTIONS OF FOUR SELECTED SAVINGS AND LOAN INSTITUTIONS, 1988

	Lamar Savings Association	American Diversified Savings Bank	Bell Savings and Loan Association	Eureka Federal Savings and Loan Association
State	Texas	California	California	California
Charter at time of GAAP insolvency	State	State	State	Federal
Ownership form	Stock	Stock	Stock	Mutual
Ownership control	Closely held	Closely held	Widely held	NA
Years of ownership change	1980	1983	1982	NA
Assets at time of resolution ($ millions)	1,940	510	953	1,744
Estimated resolution cost ($ millions)	805	798	566	303
Estimated liquidation cost ($ millions)	953	798	700	396
Month of resolution	May 1988	June 1988	September 1988	May 1988
Resolution action	Southwest Plan	Insurance action	Assisted merger	Assisted merger
Years of TAP insolvency	6.25	2.5	2.5	3.75

(Table 3–11 continues)

TABLE 3-11 (continued)

	Lamar Savings Association	American Diversified Savings Bank	Bell Savings and Loan Association	Eureka Federal Savings and Loan Association
Direct investment to assets (%)[a]	15.8	69.7	2.6	0.4
Brokered deposits to assets (%)[b]	3.2	35.4	5.2	0.7
Acquisition and development loans to assets (%)[c]	3.0	0.1	2.4	0.4
Real estate held to assets (%)[d]	9.2	24.9	1.7	0.0
Average annual growth rate of assets, 1983–1985 (%)	63.1	346.3	48.0	17.1
Year placed in Management Consignment Program	NA	1986	1985	NA

NA = not applicable.

a. Industry average = 0.5 percent.
b. Industry average = 1.8 percent.
c. Industry average = 2.0 percent.
d. Industry average = 1.8 percent.
SOURCE: Federal Home Loan Bank Board.

it was found years ago that

> The character of the ownership and control of the smaller unit banks has not been such as to promote sound banking. From the point of view of ownership, the local bank has generally been the affair of a relatively small number of inhabitants; from the point of view of control, it has been in a substantial number of cases a one-man or one-family bank. The failure of many banks may be directly ascribed to the abuses which grew out of this situation (Bremer 1935, 110).

The Cost of Cleaning Up the Mess

One of the more controversial issues in the savings and loan problem concerns recognizing and acknowledging its size. Many contend that the FHLBB was slow, perhaps deliberately so, to recognize and acknowledge that the taxpayers would be required to pay the cost of the cleanup. It is, therefore, important to discuss the official estimated cost of resolving insolvent savings and loans and how this cost has changed over time. Since a significant portion of this cost is borne by the Treasury Department, we should also understand how tax benefits to acquirers of troubled savings and loans affect the estimates of the cleanup cost.

Alternative Cost Estimates

Table 3–12 presents information on the total deposits, insured deposits, and tangible capital for savings and loans; the total reserves and contingent liabilities (associated with troubled institutions) for the FSLIC; the number and assets of the open but tangible-insolvent savings and loans; and the estimated present-value cost for resolving insolvent savings and loans as a percentage of their total assets over the period 1980–1988. As we know, the high interest rates of the late 1970s and early 1980s drove the savings and loan industry into insolvency. That is to say, if one marked-to-market all the fixed-rate mortgages on the books of savings and loans at the time, the resulting write-downs would have exceeded the tangible capital in the industry. Such calculations were actually made in the early 1980s and did indeed indicate the insolvency of the industry. As table 3–12 shows, how-

69

TABLE 3–12
Taxpayer Protections in the Form of Savings and Loans' Capital and the FSLIC's Reserves, 1980–1988

	Savings and Loans ($ billions)			FSLIC ($ billions)		Insolvent Savings and Loans[a]		Estimated Resolution Cost as a Percentage of Total Assets[b]
	Total deposits	Insured deposits	Tangible capital	Total reserves	Contingent liability	Number	Assets ($ billions)	
1980	503	483	32	6.5	0	43	0.4	11.5
1981	520	498	25	6.2	0	112	29	5.5
1982	560	534	4	6.3	0	415	220	4.5
1983	671	626	4	6.4	0	515	234	5.9
1984	784	720	3	5.6	0	695	336	14.6
1985	844	780	9	4.6	1.6	705	335	17.5
1986	891	824	15	(6.3)	10.5	672	324	24.6
1987	933	855	9	(13.7)	17.4	672	336	34.7
1988	972	888	23	(75.0)	24.2	508	283	31.0

a. Tangible-insolvent institutions still unresolved at year-end.
b. Estimated present-value cost to resolve insolvent institutions as a percentage of the assets of the resolved institutions during the year.
SOURCE: Federal Home Loan Bank Board.

ever, even the strictest or most conservative accounting measure indicated that the industry was solvent, though barely so, from 1982 through 1984 when tangible capital was only $3–$4 billion in a three-quarter trillion dollar industry. Despite the significant decline in capital, however, both total and insured deposits at savings and loans increased. The risk exposure of the FSLIC was therefore increasing too insofar as industry capital was being depleted and its own reserves were declining. Worse yet, the number and assets of insolvent institutions were both increasing throughout most of the 1980s. Furthermore, the estimated present-value cost of resolving insolvent institutions as a percentage of their assets was growing significantly over the period as the problem in the industry switched from an interest-rate spread problem to an asset-quality problem.

It was not until 1985, however, that the FSLIC and its auditor, the General Accounting Office (GAO), first recognized and acknowledged that the annual financial statements of the FSLIC should reflect a contingent liability for troubled savings and loans. As stated in the 1985 *Annual Report* of the FHLBB,

> Prior to 1985, the Corporation considered it impractical to estimate its contingent liability for those troubled institutions that would likely require new or increased financial assistance. . . . As of December 31, 1985, the Corporation . . . estimated a contingent liability for troubled institutions that it believes will likely require new or increased financial assistance in the near term. . . . [It] focused on near term losses, and is not a projection of resolving all future problems in the savings and loan industry (*Annual Report*, Federal Home Loan Bank Board, 1985).

The amount of the contingent liability, as shown in table 3–15, was $1.6 billion. It rose sharply thereafter, driving the FSLIC itself into insolvency. Until this contingent liability had to be booked beginning in 1985, the FHLBB had no specific reason to provide an official estimate of the size of the problem. From then on, however, the pressure was on the FHLBB not only to provide a figure but also to defend it.

Figure 3–2 estimates the present-value cost of resolving troubled institutions by the FHLBB, which eventually went considerably beyond the narrow contingent liability recorded on the

71

FIGURE 3–2
SELECTED COST ESTIMATES OF RESOLVING INSOLVENT SAVINGS AND
LOANS, JUNE 1985–MARCH 1989

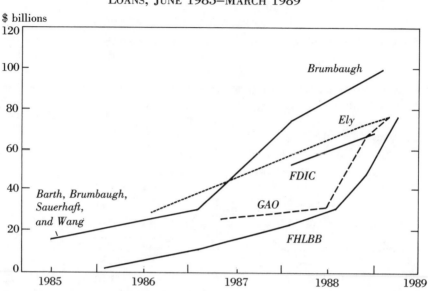

SOURCE: Adapted from Wall (1989).

FSLIC's books. The figure also shows the costs estimated by selected others as well. The official estimate of the FHLBB has always been below the unofficial estimates of others, even though all the estimates increased greatly over time. Each of the estimates will now be discussed in turn.

The Federal Home Loan Bank Board. The FHLBB's December 1985 estimate of $1.6 billion was a contingent liability for troubled institutions that the bank board believed would likely require financial assistance in the near term. The figure was based on the FSLIC's historical loss experience and an evaluation of the past and present financial condition of the troubled institutions. This methodology focused on near-term losses and did not project the cost of resolving all future problems in the industry. The FHLBB's December 1986 estimate of $10.5 billion included only those institutions in the FSLIC caseload as of December 31, 1986. This figure represented the estimated present value of the total cost to provide the most probable form of assistance in each case less any costs already recognized because of some existing FSLIC assistance. The FHLBB's December 1987 estimate of $22.7 billion or more included a contingent liability of $17.4 billion for future assistance to troubled institutions that was both probable and estimable and the costs (at least $5.3 billion) to resolve an additional 300 GAAP-insolvent institutions. The contingent liability included bid prices received by the FSLIC and the estimable and probable resolution costs of the remaining savings and loans in the FSLIC caseload, plus an additional allowance for institutions located in the Southwest that were not part of the FSLIC caseload as of December 31, 1987. The FHLBB's mid-year estimate of $30.9 billion revised the December 31, 1987, estimate upward by $8.2 billion for institutions in the Southwest based on an analysis of actual resolution costs on Southwest cases compared with year-end estimates. The FHLBB's October 1988 estimate was a range, $45–50 billion, based on all unresolved institutions in the FSLIC's caseload as of October 1, 1988, plus all other savings and loans that were GAAP-insolvent in June 1988 but not in the FSLIC's caseload. Using its experience in resolving savings and loans during the first three quarters of the year, the FHLBB estimated a range of costs for the resolution of future FSLIC cases, $24.9–29.9 billion. To this was added the estimated $20 billion in FSLIC notes and guarantees under assistance agreements of previously resolved cases. The FHLBB's February 1989 estimate was a range, $75–80 billion. (All of this information was reported in M. D. Wall 1989.)

The General Accounting Office. The GAO's January 1989 estimate was at least $77 billion, of which $37 billion was for institutions that had already been resolved and $40 billion was for institutions that had not yet been resolved. The GAO's May 1988 estimate was a range, $26–36 billion, and was based on the December 1987 financial audit. The GAO's estimates based on 1988 data were intended to include the costs of 1988 FSLIC actions to date that had been assumed by the FSLIC. The GAO's October 1988 estimate for the costs of resolving institutions that were insolvent at the end of September was a range, $45–50 billion, to which $19.9 billion of FSLIC's provisions for losses and notes payable was added. Thus, the October estimate ranged from $64.9–69.9 billion. The GAO's March 1987 estimate is taken from its report to Congress in which the GAO stated that given its "knowledge of the condition in the industry, we do not believe that $25 billion overstates the extent of the problem facing FSLIC."

The Federal Deposit Insurance Corporation. The FDIC's estimates include the costs of handling resolved institutions plus institutions that were unprofitable *and* insolvent. Institutions are insolvent for these estimates if the sum of tangible capital, loan loss reserves, and general valuation allowances is less than zero. The FDIC reduces the asset values at insolvent and unprofitable institutions by comparing the book value of these assets with the corresponding book values of a related group of peer institutions. The liabilities of the insolvent and unprofitable institutions are then subtracted from the adjusted asset values to obtain a cost estimate for resolving these institutions. The FDIC's December 1987 estimate of $52.8 billion was based on 489 insolvent and unprofitable institutions holding assets of $209 billion. The FDIC's November 1988 estimate of $68.9 billion was based on 134 resolved institutions through October 20, 1988, and 396 troubled institutions holding $167 billion in assets not yet resolved. The FDIC's November estimate was split between FSLIC's books, $24.8 billion, and the resolved institutions.

Barth, Brumbaugh, Sauerhaft, and Wang. All four of these individuals were at the FHLBB during the spring of 1985 and prepared, presented, and subsequently published a paper in which they estimated the cost at the time of resolving the 434 GAAP-insolvent institutions at $15.8 billion (see Barth, Brumbaugh, Sauerhaft, and Wang 1985; and Anderson 1985, A-16). Bank Board Chairman Edwin J. Gray, however, in answering questions about the report, "emphasized that it painted a worst-case scenario which was very unlikely to occur" (Crutsinger 1985). Subsequently, Gray stated:

> Last Spring, I estimated the cost of resolving known cases requiring FSLIC assistance to be in the neighborhood of $16 billion. A good deal of work has gone into a revision of last year's estimate and we now put the known cost at $19.5 billion. There are borderline cases, however, which I want to add to this estimate which would bring the total cost to $23.5 billion (Gray 1987, 5).

74

In any event, R. Dan Brumbaugh, Jr., a senior fellow at the Center for Economic Policy Research at Stanford University, continued to provide cost estimates of resolving insolvent savings and loans. His December 1986 estimate of $30 billion, like the earlier estimate with Barth, Sauerhaft, and Wang, included only the cost of resolving insolvent institutions. His December 1987 estimate of $75 billion and January 1989 estimate of $100 billion, however, were broadened to include the costs of resolving solvent but troubled institutions.

Ely. Bert Ely, a consultant based in Alexandria, Virginia, has calculated the simple average of the marked-down value of assets and the capitalized value of gross interest income. Estimates before May 1988 are based on the capitalized gross interest income stream. Ely's September 1987 estimate of "at least $52 billion" was based on the March 1987 balance sheet data for savings and loans. Ely's September 1988 estimate was a range, $70–75 billion, 20–25 percent of which was on the books of the FSLIC. Ely's January 1989 estimate was a range, $75–80 billion, half of which was on the FSLIC's books. The last two estimates were based on June 1988 financial data for the savings and loan industry.

Clearly, estimates regarding the present-value cost of cleaning up the mess in the savings and loan industry have varied widely. Although all the estimates increased over time, the official estimate was always the lowest. Finally, however, only a few days after his inauguration President Bush recognized and acknowledged that the cost was so enormous that taxpayers would have to share in its burden. At that time the official estimate of resolving all the troubled savings and loans in 1989 and beyond was about $38 billion with another $10 billion or so needed to replenish the insurance fund. The Financial Institutions Reform, Recovery and Enforcement Act (FIRREA) therefore provided $50 billion for this effort. Not long afterward, however, the cost estimates continued their escalation. As table 3–13 shows, the $50 billion was considered far too little not long after August 1989. Indeed, even the Treasury Department raised the official cost estimate to $89–132 billion in May 1990. One can truly say that the worst financial disaster in the history of the world has occurred.

Strangely, though, these estimates are not all-inclusive because they do not fully capture the tax benefits flowing to acquirers and others when troubled savings and loans are resolved.

TABLE 3-13

SELECTED ESTIMATES OF THE COST OF RESOLVING THE SAVINGS AND LOAN CRISIS, 1989–1990
(billions of dollars)

Source of Estimate	Estimated Cost	Description
OMB (February 1989)	40	The ten-year net budget outlays.
OMB (February 1989)	158	The gross federal cash outlays 1989–1999, including all FSLIC Resolution Fund, RTC, and SAIF expenditures plus repayment of pre-FY1989 FSLIC notes and federal interest on REFCORP bonds.
OMB (August 1989)	203	Same as above, adjusted for changes in financing made in conference, plus federal interest on the REFCORP bonds through 2021.
GAO (July 1989)	257	The gross federal and nonfederal cash flows of restoring failed savings and loans and establishing SAIF over a thirty-three-year period, including repayment of pre-FY1989 FSLIC notes and tax losses.

Source	Estimate	Description
CBO (August 1990)	287	The thirty-three-year federal and nonfederal cash outflows, including repayment of pre-FY1989 FSLIC notes and interest on Treasury Department borrowing but net of liquidation proceeds.
CBO (March 1990)	75–80	Net costs of the RTC caseload.
GAO (April 1990)	325[a]	Reestimate of previous GAO estimate using GAO, not OMB, assumptions.
GAO (April 1990)	140[a]	Present-value estimate of the above estimate provided by Comptroller General Bowsher in written testimony.
Ely (April 1990)	75	Present-value estimate that excludes $50 billion for the pre-1989 resolutions.
Barth-Brumbaugh (April 1990)	91–135	Present-value estimate that excludes the pre-1989 resolutions. The estimate depends on the resolution costs per dollar of assets of resolved institutions.
Treasury Department (May 1990)	89–132	Present-value estimate of insurance losses in the RTC caseload under a range of assumptions that excludes the pre-1989 resolutions.

a. At least.
SOURCE: Adapted from the Floor Statement of Senator Donald W. Riegle, Jr., June 11, 1990, p. 44.

In particular, special FSLIC tax provisions were enacted as part of the Economic Recovery Tax Act of 1981, with these provisions: (1) supervisory mergers are tax-free; (2) depositors are treated as shareholders for purposes of applying net operating loss carryover limitations to supervisory savings and loan mergers; (3) bad debt reserves are prevented from recapture when an assisted institution repays the FSLIC; and (4) the FSLIC financial assistance is excluded from taxable income of the recipient institution, and no write-down is required in the tax basis of assets of the institution. The FHLBB considered these tax benefits as a way to avoid liquidations and to reduce the pressure on the FSLIC's financial resources from 1980 through 1988. Indeed, the FHLBB successfully opposed the tax bill passed by the House of Representatives in December 1985 that would have repealed these special tax rules, effective for supervisory mergers or acquisitions occurring on or after January 1, 1986, and for FSLIC assistance payments received in taxable years of an institution beginning on or after January 1, 1986. Because the FSLIC's reserves were declining throughout the 1980s, it was incumbent upon the FHLBB to engage in cost-effective resolutions. As an agency of the federal government, however, the bank board also had to consider the all-inclusive cost of any resolution, the cost both to the FSLIC and to the Department of Treasury. Since the FHLBB was required by statute not to permit FSLIC assistance in a particular case to exceed the cost of a liquidation, the tax benefits could easily influence the choice whether to sell or to liquidate an institution. More specifically, the tax attributes of a savings and loan acquired in a tax-free merger or conversion normally survive in full after the transaction. This tax-free status allows savings and loans to carry net operating losses, losses that were incurred but not utilized, back ten years and forward five years, after an acquisition. They are also not required to have the tax basis for the assets taken over in a merger set equal to their fair market value at the date of merger. That is, the built-in losses will include the accrued, "paper" losses reflected in the portfolio of low-interest mortgages currently worth less than the original amounts but not yet deducted for tax purposes. Furthermore, the interest on FSLIC notes and the yield maintenance payments are excludable from taxable income. Thus when the built-in losses are deducted for tax purposes and the loss is then reimbursed by the FSLIC, the reimbursement is not taxable.

4

The Financial Institutions Reform, Recovery, and Enforcement Act

The Financial Institutions Reform, Recovery, and Enforcement Act was signed into law on August 9, 1989, six months after President Bush announced his plan to resolve the savings and loan crisis. As appendix E shows, considerable controversy and delay occurred before enactment of the last major piece of financial legislation in the 1980s, with the president even threatening a veto at one point in the process. In any event, at the time the FIRREA was enacted, the announced goals were to resolve insolvent savings and loans efficiently, improve the financial condition of the federal deposit insurance funds, and restore safety and soundness to federally insured depository institutions. Although the major impetus behind the FIRREA was the widely recognized need to provide funds to resolve open but insolvent savings and loans, the law also fundamentally changed the regulatory and supervisory structure of the industry and reversed the trend toward liberalizing their powers. The major issue is whether the reforms embodied in the FIRREA will prevent a similar debacle from ever again occurring.

Overview of the FIRREA

The major features of the FIRREA can be conveniently grouped into five broad categories. First, the regulatory and supervisory structure for the savings and loan industry was significantly changed by placing the primary regulator and supervisor of the

NOTE: This chapter draws heavily on Barth, Benston, and Wiest (1990).

industry within the Treasury Department and the insurance fund for savings and loans under the administration of the Federal Deposit Insurance Corporation. Second, a broad-based funding program was provided to resolve open but insolvent savings and loans, to replenish the deposit insurance fund for savings and loans, and to strengthen the insurance fund for commercial banks. At the same time restrictions on switching from a savings and loan charter to a commercial bank charter were adopted to control better which of the two separate insurance funds would receive the deposit insurance premiums. Third, housing programs were established through funding from the FHL banks to member institutions for long-term, low- and moderate-income, owner-occupied, and affordable rental housing. Fourth, new and more stringent restrictions were imposed on the activities of both state and federally insured savings and loans, and new and higher capital requirements were statutorily imposed. Finally, the FIRREA substantially strengthened the formal enforcement powers available to the regulators and supervisors of savings and loans and commercial banks and granted the Justice Department significantly greater power for use against any persons involved in misconduct relating to the activities of these institutions.

To understand the effect these changes mandated by the FIRREA will have on the savings and loan industry, we should take a closer look at each of them.

Regulatory Structure. The FIRREA abolished the FSLIC, making the FDIC the sole administrator of the federal deposit insurance system for savings and loans and commercial banks, with two separate insurance funds—the Savings Association Insurance Fund, which replaces the FSLIC, and the Bank Insurance Fund, which replaces the Permanent Insurance Fund. The rationale for this particular structural change was the belief that the goals of the regulator as an industry advocate and as an insurer inherently conflicted. (As a historical aside, in the 1960s Congress considered various proposals to place the FSLIC and the FDIC under a single agency called the Federal Deposit and Savings Insurance Board.) The FIRREA also abolished the FHLBB, replacing it with the Office of Thrift Supervision (OTS). The OTS became a bureau within the Treasury Department, with regulatory and supervisory powers for savings and loans comparable with those of the Office of the Comptroller of the Currency. Unlike

80

the comptroller of the currency, however, the OTS retains authority over both federally and state-chartered institutions, although the FDIC is authorized to take enforcement action against savings and loans, even over OTS objection. This enforcement authority is in addition to the power to terminate insurance for savings and loans, which the FDIC may also do notwithstanding any objection from the OTS. The Board of Directors of the FDIC, however, was expanded from three to five members, including the comptroller of the currency and the director of the OTS. Placing the OTS within the Treasury Department, it was believed, would insulate the regulator from industry pressures. In addition, the FIRREA established a new independent agency, the Federal Housing Finance Board, to replace the FHLBB as the regulator and supervisor of the twelve district FHL banks. The Federal Housing Finance Board, managed by five directors, includes the secretary of the Department of Housing and Urban Development (HUD) and four private citizens appointed by the president and subject to confirmation by the Senate.

Resolution of Insolvent Savings and Loans and Restrictions on Charter Switches. The FIRREA established a new fund, the FSLIC Resolution Fund, to assume all the liabilities of the FSLIC associated with the insolvent savings and loans resolved before January 1, 1988, and the Resolution Trust Corporation to resolve the insolvent savings and loans placed into conservatorship or receivership between January 1, 1989, and August 9, 1992. Funding for the FSLIC Resolution Fund comes from the sale to investors of Financing Corporation bonds—an entity established by the Competitive Equality Banking Act of 1987— assessments on institutions insured by the Savings Association Insurance Fund through 1991, and the Treasury Department. Funding for the Resolution Trust Corporation is arranged by the Resolution Funding Corporation and by the Treasury Department. The Resolution Trust Corporation is managed by the FDIC under the general supervision of a five-member oversight board that consists of the secretary of the Treasury as chairperson, the chairman of the Board of Governors of the Federal Reserve System, the secretary of HUD, and two private citizens appointed by the president and subject to confirmation by the Senate. The corporation was also charged with disposing of the Federal Asset Disposition Association within 180 days of the date of enactment of the FIRREA and reviewing all FSLIC resolutions in 1988 and 1989 to determine whether any costs could be saved by restructuring those transactions within the terms of their governing agreements.

The FIRREA provided funding of $50 billion, based on the administration's present-value estimate that about $40 billion was needed by the Resolution Trust Corporation to resolve open but insolvent savings and loans and $10 billion to replenish the savings and loan insurance fund. This amount is in addition to the nearly $40 billion that the FHLBB estimated it cost to resolve 223 savings and loans in 1988. Of this amount, $20 billion was raised in September 1989, with $1.2 billion coming from the retained earnings of the FHL banks and $18.8 billion from the sale of government debt by the Treasury Department. The remaining $30 billion would come from the periodic sale of the private debt by the Resolution Funding Corporation through early 1991. None of this funding affects the Gramm-Rudman-Hollings deficit constraint. The FHL banks would be assessed an additional $1.375 billion against their retained earnings during 1990 and 1991 to help decrease the principal of the debt issued by the Resolution Funding Corporation. Interest payments on the debt would be paid, in part, by assessments not to exceed $300 million per year on the FHL banks. Because the Treasury Department will pay the remaining balance, these particular interest payments will be on-budget and therefore subject to the Gramm-Rudman-Hollings deficit constraint.

The FIRREA specifies that both the Savings Association Insurance Fund and the Bank Insurance Fund should increase reserves until they equal 1.25 percent of insured deposits, or even up to a maximum of 1.50 percent, if the FDIC deems it appropriate. To achieve these targeted ratios, higher deposit insurance premiums were imposed on both savings and loans and commercial banks. More specifically, whereas institutions insured by the Savings Association Insurance Fund were assessed at 0.208 percent of total deposits before the FIRREA, in effect throughout 1990, the assessment rate increases to 0.23 percent from January 1, 1991, through December 31, 1993, and then decreases to 0.18 percent from January 1, 1994, through December 31, 1997. The assessment rate will be 0.15 percent thereafter. Institutions insured by the Bank Insurance Fund were assessed at a rate of 0.083 percent of total domestic deposits before the FIRREA. On

January 1, 1990, the rate increased to 0.12 percent, and then beginning on January 1, 1991, the rate increases to 0.15 percent and remains at that level thereafter so that institutions under the insurance funds will be at parity beginning in 1998. To restore the ratio of targeted reserves to insured deposits to 1.25 percent in the event of significant losses, the FDIC may increase premiums to a maximum assessment rate of 0.325 percent at a maximum annual increase of 0.075 percent. These conditions became operative in August 1990 when the FDIC announced that the premiums for commercial banks would be increased to 0.195 percent in 1991 rather than the initially scheduled increase of 0.15 percent, which will represent a 135 percent increase in assessment rates since 1989.

The FIRREA generally eases the restrictions on the ability of a savings and loan to convert to a bank charter, to sell deposits or branches to commercial banks, or to be acquired by bank holding companies. More specifically, deposits may be transferred from the coverage of the Savings Association Insurance Fund to the coverage of the Bank Insurance Fund, so long as the conversion affects no more than 35 percent of the total deposits of each institution participating in the conversion or the conversion occurs in connection with the acquisition of a troubled institution insured by the savings association fund. The so-called Oakar Amendment, moreover, allows a bank holding company to acquire a savings and loan—even healthy institutions and not just troubled institutions as permitted since 1982—and merge it into a commercial bank subsidiary insured by the Bank Insurance Fund, with the resulting institution having some of its deposits insured by the savings association fund and some by the bank fund. Restrictions on tandem operations are also lifted, so that commercial banks may cross-market their services and products through acquired savings and loan branch offices in other states. Several provisions in the FIRREA, however, may inhibit the conversion of savings and loan deposits to bank deposits. Although a savings and loan may switch charters, a five-year moratorium on deposit insurance conversions from the savings association fund to the bank fund by healthy savings and loans prevents them from evading the higher premiums for the savings association fund. Furthermore, deposit conversions between the two insurance funds are subject to exit and entrance fees. Initially, a ninety-basis-point exit fee had to be paid to the savings association fund and an eighty-basis-point entry fee paid to the bank fund. The FDIC, which sets these fees, reduced the bank fund entrance fee to sixty basis points in the spring of 1990, however. If deposits are converted to a bank-chartered institution without changing insurance funds, the higher premiums for savings association insurance must be paid until the five-year moratorium ends, at which time the exit and entrance fees may be paid and all ties to the Savings Association Insurance Fund ended.

Affordable Housing. The FIRREA expands funding for affordable housing by requiring each FHL bank to subsidize the interest rate on advances to member institutions engaged in lending for long-term, low- and moderate-income, owner-occupied, and affordable rental housing. Specifically, for each year 1990 through 1993, the FHL banks are required to contribute 5 percent of their annual net income, with a minimum of $50 million to this affordable housing program. In 1994, the requirement rises to 6 percent, with a minimum of $75 million. From 1995 on, the requirement rises still further to 10 percent of net income, with a minimum of $100 million. The advances are to be used specifically to finance home ownership by families with incomes at or below 80 percent of the median income in the area or to finance the purchase, construction, or rehabilitation of rental housing, at least 20 percent of the units of which will be occupied by and affordable for very low-income households, defined as households with incomes below 50 percent of the median income for the area.

Restrictions on Savings and Loan Activities and Higher Capital Requirements. The FIRREA restricted the type and extent of activities in which savings and loans may engage, reversing the liberalizing trend in the federal and state legislation enacted in the late 1970s and early 1980s. Insured state-chartered institutions are restricted to those activities and amounts permitted federally chartered savings and loans, unless the FDIC finds that the activity does not pose a significant risk to the insurance fund and those institutions engaged in the activity are in compliance with the fully phased-in capital requirements. Insured institutions and their subsidiaries are also prohibited from investing in corporate debt securities that, when acquired, are not rated in one of the four highest rating categories by at least one nationally recognized rating organization (so-called junk bonds). An exception is made for mutual savings and loans, which may acquire junk bonds but only through separately capitalized subsidiaries and only for certain bonds. Furthermore, a savings and loan may transfer any junk bonds to its holding company or a holding company affiliate in return for a "qualified note." The divestiture of all existing junk bonds held by savings and loans is required as quickly as prudent, but not later than July 1, 1994.

Nonresidential or commercial real estate loans are restricted to four times capital, rather than the pre-FIRREA limit of 40 percent of assets. This new restriction reduces permissible holdings for all institutions whose capital is less than 10 percent of assets. The law does not require the divestiture of any commercial loans that were legal when made, however. With limited exceptions, savings and loans cannot make loans to one borrower that exceed 15 percent of its capital, with an additional 10 percent for fully secured loans; this limitation also applies to national banks. Furthermore, the FDIC may restrict savings and loans from engaging in any activity deemed to pose a significant risk to the Savings Association Insurance Fund. The FDIC may also grant exceptions to some restrictions, but only for institutions that meet the fully phased-in capital requirements.

The Qualified Thrift Lender test was tightened, requiring savings and loans to hold at least 70 percent—up from 60 percent—of all portfolio assets (mainly tangible assets) in qualified (primarily housing-related) investments after July 1, 1991. Within specified limits, double credit in meeting this requirement is granted for starter home developments and for residential, church, school, nursing home, and small business loans made in designated areas in which the credit needs of lower-income residents are not being adequately met as determined by the Office of Thrift Supervision. Savings and loans that fail to become or remain qualified thrift lenders are required either to become a commercial bank or to be limited to those activities permitted a national bank.

The FIRREA also prevents depository institutions that do not meet minimum capital requirements from accepting any brokered deposits, effective 120 days after the day of enactment. Although the FIRREA did not impose maximum loan-to-value limits on real estate loans, the federal banking agencies were directed to implement general limits for both savings and loans and commercial banks. In contrast to tighter restrictions in general, savings and loans were authorized to issue demand deposit accounts to all individuals and businesses, not just to businesses in which they had a preexisting credit relationship. As is the case for commercial banks, however, no interest may be paid on these accounts.

Considered by many as perhaps the most important provision of the FIRREA for preventing future problems, a three-tiered system of new and higher capital requirements for savings and loans was statutorily imposed. First, a savings and loan must have tangible capital equal to at least 1.5 percent of assets. Tangible capital is defined as core capital less any "intangible assets" as defined by the Office of the Comptroller of the Currency, but including purchased mortgage servicing rights up to a limit determined by the FDIC. Second, a savings and loan must have core capital equal to at least 3 percent of assets. Core capital is defined by the Office of the Comptroller of the Currency, but savings and loans may include any supervisory goodwill—goodwill that resulted from the acquisition of troubled institutions during the 1980s—that they held on April 12, 1989, up to 1.5 percent of assets before January 1, 1992, then being phased out over several years and eliminated altogether after December 31, 1994. Third, the new risk-based capital requirements imposed on savings and loans may incorporate both the credit risk and the interest-rate risk of their portfolios. Although the requirements are set by the Office of Thrift Supervision, any deviations from the risk-based capital requirements for national banks must not result in materially less capital for savings and loans than for national banks.

Before January 1, 1991, the Office of Thrift Supervision may restrict the asset growth of—and must require a plan of compliance from—savings and loans that do not meet these new capital standards. After that date, restrictions on asset growth will be mandatory, and limitations may be imposed on the payment of dividends or compensation until the requirements are met. The FIRREA also provides for the appointment of a conservator or receiver for any institution that has substantially insufficient capital or fails to comply with its submitted business plan. Furthermore, all the financial regulatory agencies for savings and loans and commercial banks must establish uniform accounting standards within one year of the day of enactment.

Enforcement and Supervision. The FIRREA greatly expands

and enhances the enforcement powers of savings and loan regulators and supervisors as well as those of the Department of Justice. The scope of individuals covered by the enforcement provisions, moreover, is broadened to cover all "institution-affiliated parties," including directors, officers, employees, controlling stockholders, and independent contractors, such as attorneys, appraisers, and accountants. In addition, the enforcement powers extend to savings and loan holding companies, subsidiaries of savings and loan holding companies, and service corporations. The FIRREA provides for increased power to issue final cease-and-desist orders, while lowering the standards to issue temporary orders. An order may include restrictions on asset growth and on specific activities by an institution or its employees. Such orders may also be issued whenever the books and records of an institution are so incomplete that the regulator cannot determine its financial condition. Regulators have enough power to remove or suspend directors, officers, or other "institution-affiliated" parties from savings and loans and to impose a ban on their employment in any federally insured depository institution, any banking regulatory agency, any FHL bank, or the Resolution Trust Corporation. The FIRREA allows the imposition of civil penalties for virtually any form of misconduct, fines for which range from $5,000 per day for unintended violations to $1,000,000 per day for knowing or reckless violations causing a substantial loss. The failure to submit or publish reports or the submission of incomplete, false, or misleading reports could lead to fines ranging from $2,000 to $1,000,000 per day depending on the severity of the violation. The Department of Justice is also given expanded authority to penalize abuses relating to insured depository institutions, with criminal penalties up to $1,000,000 in fines and imprisonment up to twenty years for certain offenses. (As a historical aside, Willis Parker and John Chapman, writing in 1934, observed, "It was recommended by the first comptroller [of the currency] that the failure of a national bank be declared prima facie fraudulent and that the officers and directors be made personally responsible as well as punishable criminally unless upon investigation it was found that the bank's affairs had been honestly administered" [Willis and Chapman 1934, 201]).

The Office of Thrift Supervision can more easily and in a more timely manner appoint a conservator or receiver for troubled savings and loans, an extremely important function because most institutions resolved were insolvent for years before resolution. A new ground for appointment is that the institution has incurred or is likely to incur losses that will deplete all or substantially all of its capital and that the institution has no reasonable prospect for replenishment of the capital without federal assistance. Furthermore, having substantially insufficient capital may now be deemed an unsafe and unsound condition and hence could lead to the appointment of a conservator or receiver. The FDIC or the Resolution Trust Corporation may be appointed the conservator, while the corporation shall be appointed receiver during the three years following enactment of the FIRREA and the FDIC thereafter. As conservator or receiver, the FDIC or the Resolution Trust Corporation can permit the merger of a savings and loan with any other savings and loan or commercial bank without the approval of the other federal banking agencies.

The FIRREA provides for expedited termination of deposit insurance by significantly reducing the time in which an institution must correct the condition or conduct giving rise to the action for termination of insurance. Completely new provisions are also provided so that insurance may be temporarily suspended if an institution is found to have no tangible capital.

The FIRREA also specifies cross-guaranty provisions that empower the FDIC to obtain reimbursement from any of a holding company's commonly controlled insured depository institutions, if the FDIC incurs a loss from liquidating or selling a troubled institution.

Effects of the FIRREA on Savings and Loans

In three areas the FIRREA directly affects savings and loans and the FHL banks—funding provisions, activity restrictions, and capital requirements. Each will be discussed.

Funding Provisions. Savings and loans are now directly assessed to pay the operating expenses of the Office of Thrift Supervision. Previously, the FHLBB was funded by FSLIC premiums and, to a lesser extent, by assessments on the FHL banks, which represented indirect charges on savings and loans. Although the FIRREA may not, therefore, impose additional regulatory operating costs on the savings and loan industry, those costs are certainly more explicit. Furthermore, an increasingly smaller number of institutions are bearing those costs as the Resolution Trust Corporation resolves insolvent institutions and thereby shrinks the size of the savings and loan industry. The Office of Thrift Supervision is therefore under considerable pressure to reduce its operating costs in line with the consolidation occurring in the industry and with the operating costs of other financial regulatory agencies.

More important, savings and loans will pay higher deposit insurance premiums to replenish the insurance fund. Based on deposit levels for the 2,533 GAAP-solvent institutions in June 1989, the higher premiums cost savings and loans roughly $800 million more per year through 1993 than if they paid the same scheduled premiums as commercial banks. Furthermore, the savings and loan industry will bear indirectly a significant portion of the burden of funding the Resolution Trust Corporation and the affordable housing initiatives through its stock ownership in the FHL banks. When all costs are phased in, the FHL bank expenses are estimated to increase by $500 million per year (see Barth, Benston, and Weist 1990). Based upon the 80 percent dividend payout for 1989, then, payments to member institutions would be $400 million per year less.

The opening of FHL bank membership to federally insured commercial banks and credit unions that hold 10 percent or more of their assets in residential loans and related assets may improve the earnings opportunities of the FHL banks. There were, however, relatively few new members in the system by the summer of 1990. Institutions have hesitated to join because, once becoming members, they must purchase stock equal to either 1 percent of their residential loans and mortgage-backed securities or 0.3 percent of total assets, whichever is greater. Yet, the FHL bank stock is not a marketable security; instead it is bought and sold by the FHL banks at its par value of $100 per share. Stockholders, however, do receive quarterly dividends on their investment. Potential and existing members are concerned that dividends may be reduced as advances decline when insolvent savings and loans are resolved and as capital-deficient institutions shrink to meet the higher capital requirements. In addition, some worry that still further resources of the FHL banks may be tapped to resolve the savings and loan problems. To support these concerns, during the first six months of 1990, total advances declined $36 billion or 22 percent, and the dividend rate was reduced to 9.26 percent, down from 11.0 percent in 1989. Beyond these effects, the change in the scope of membership should reduce the relative value of a savings and loan charter, because those institutions will no longer have sole access to FHL bank advances. To forestall state-chartered savings and loans from withdrawing from the FHL bank system, in August 1990 the FDIC decided to "make no assurances" that institutions that withdrew would be permitted to maintain their federal insurance. A final decision was to be made in eighteen months after the issue was considered in conjunction with other regulators. The FIRREA made it clear that federally chartered institutions must maintain their membership but left the status of state-chartered institutions unclear.

Activity Restrictions. Although the FIRREA prohibits savings and loans from holding junk bonds, these particular assets accounted for less than 1 percent of industry assets and were held by only 175 savings and loans in June 1989. Three-fourths of these bonds, moreover, were held by only ten institutions. Thus, the required divestiture of these bonds over the next five years should not have a substantial effect on the entire industry. Those savings and loans that had invested heavily in such assets, however, were encountering some difficulties, with the top three holders of junk bonds having been placed in conservatorship in 1990. The top holder reported a junk bond-to-asset ratio of 35 percent in September 1989, while the other two had ratios of 10 and 12 percent.

Restrictions on commercial real estate loans are more important to savings and loans, because most institutions hold these assets. But in June 1989 only about 200 institutions held an amount greater than 400 percent of their capital, the limit imposed by the FIRREA. These savings and loans held $5.5 billion in excess of this limit, which represents, on average, 6.2 percent of their assets.

The Qualified Thrift Lender test affects approximately one-fourth of the industry, based on balance sheets for June 1989. While the detailed data necessary to evaluate the test precisely were not available on that date, it was estimated that 78 percent of the GAAP-solvent institutions passed the test (see Barth, Benston, and Wiest 1990). Savings and loans that fail the test are not eligible for new FHL bank advances, and their investment and branching activities are restricted to the same extent as those of national banks. If institutions failing the test have not requalified within three years, they must divest themselves of ineligible investments for national banks and repay all advances, thereby losing a significant portion of the value of their charters.

Capital Requirements. The new and more stringent capital requirements will affect a significantly larger portion of the savings and loan industry than the activity restrictions. Indeed, as table 4–1 shows, 41 percent of the 2,512 GAAP-solvent institutions failed to meet one or more of the new capital requirements as of September 1989. These savings and loans, moreover, held 66 percent of industry assets. As the table shows, most of the savings and loans failing the requirements are stock-type institutions. Eleven percent of the GAAP-solvent savings and loans did not meet the 1.5 percent tangible capital requirement, and 18 percent did not meet the 3.0 percent core capital requirement; these institutions held 24 percent and 31 percent of industry assets, respectively. Thus, the new capital requirements created a substantial capital shortfall in the savings and loan industry, with 1,039 institutions holding $761 billion in assets failing to meet at least one of the new capital requirements. Without modification to the risk-based capital requirements as proposed in December 1989, as much as $22 billion of additional capital was needed by the GAAP-solvent institutions in September 1989 to meet the new requirements.

One source of potential capital is undistributed profits. On average, however, the GAAP-solvent savings and loans that failed the requirements were losing money during the first three quarters of 1989. The issuance of new stock is another potential source of capital for stock institutions, which make up 56 percent of capital-deficient savings and loans. The need for more capital may provide further incentives for mutual savings and loans to convert. The depressed conditions in the savings and loan industry and the troubles in the Middle East that arose in the summer of 1990, however, were significant barriers to the issuance of stock.

Selling assets is the other method of meeting higher capital requirements, but only those whose market values are above their book values can be useful for this purpose. In particular, the sale of branches or subsidiary investments has occurred at some of the capital-deficient savings and loans. The relaxation of restric-

TABLE 4–1

BALANCE SHEETS OF GAAP-SOLVENT SAVINGS AND LOAN INSTITUTIONS FAILING AND PASSING THE NEW CAPITAL REQUIREMENTS, BY OWNERSHIP TYPE, SEPTEMBER 1989

Item	Mutual-owned Savings and Loans		Stock-owned Savings and Loans		All GAAP-Solvent
	Passing	Failing	Passing	Failing	
	Percentage of Total Gross Assets				
Mortgage assets, total	76.5	69.8	78.1	68.9	71.9
Mortgage loans	65.9	55.3	60.5	52.4	56.0
Residential mortgage loans	61.5	48.2	54.6	43.4	48.5
Commercial mortgage loans	4.4	7.1	5.9	8.9	7.5
Land loans	0.6	1.3	1.3	1.7	1.4
Mortgage-backed securities	10.1	13.2	16.3	14.8	14.4
Nonmortgage assets, total	4.2	6.8	5.3	7.9	6.8
Consumer loans	3.6	5.2	4.4	4.3	4.4
Commercial loans	0.6	1.6	0.9	3.6	2.4
Cash and securities	15.2	13.5	10.4	12.6	12.5
Direct investment[a]	1.0	1.8	1.9	2.8	2.3
Repossessed assets	0.3	2.6	0.6	2.1	1.6
Other assets	2.7	5.6	3.7	5.7	4.9
Total assets (gross)	100.0	100.0	100.0	100.0	100.0

		Percentage of Total Liabilities			
Deposits, total	93.8	81.2	74.7	70.8	75.5
Insured deposits	88.1	75.6	64.5	58.9	65.5
Uninsured deposits	5.7	5.6	10.2	11.9	10.1
Managed liabilities, total	4.5	17.0	23.3	27.0	22.4
FHL bank advances	2.6	10.7	9.6	12.5	10.5
Other borrowed money	1.9	6.3	13.7	14.5	11.9
Other liabilities	1.7	1.8	2.0	2.2	2.1
Total liabilities	100.0	100.0	100.0	100.0	100.0
Memo items					
Number of institutions	952	452	521	587	2,512
Gross assets ($ billions)	139.0	143.1	255.3	657.9	1,195.3
Total assets ($ billions)	136.7	139.5	249.2	636.0	1,161.4
Total liabilities ($ billions)	125.9	134.8	229.6	610.4	1,100.7
			Percentage of Total Assets		
RAP capital	8.3	4.2	8.3	4.8	5.9
GAAP capital	7.8	2.8	7.5	3.6	4.8
TAP capital	7.5	1.0	6.6	1.7	3.3
Nonperforming assets[b]	2.1	8.2	2.9	6.9	5.6
Junk bonds	0.0	0.1	0.3	1.8	1.0
Real estate held	0.1	0.4	0.3	0.4	0.4

(Table 4–1 continues)

93

TABLE 4–1 (continued)

| Item | Mutual-owned Savings and Loans | | Stock-owned Savings and Loans | | All |
	Passing	Failing	Passing	Failing	GAAP-Solvent
Service corporations	0.4	0.8	1.3	2.2	1.6
Off balance sheet items	2.6	4.3	4.3	5.2	4.6
Regulatory liquidity	11.5	7.6	7.6	6.0	7.2
	Percentage of Total Liabilities				
Brokered deposits	0.3	0.5	1.9	8.3	5.1
Repurchase agreements	1.4	3.4	6.5	7.5	6.1
Mortgage-backed bonds	0.2	1.0	1.0	1.7	1.3

NOTE: Percentages may not add to 100 as a result of rounding.

a. Direct investments include equity securities (except Federal Home Loan Bank Stock), real estate investments, and investments in service corporations or subsidiaries.

b. Nonperforming assets equal the sum of repossessed assets; deferred net losses (gains) on loans and other assets sold; goodwill and "other" intangible assets; and delinquent loans.

SOURCE: Office of Thrift Supervision.

tions on the sale of branches to commercial banks certainly enhances the benefits of this particular strategy. Apparently, savings and loans were shrinking their assets in one form or another, because in June 1989 thirty-four large savings and loans, with relatively low capital ratios, shed $8 billion in assets. More generally, industry assets declined by $100 billion during 1989.

Finally, the risk-based capital guidelines proposed by the Office of Thrift Supervision in December 1989 required less capital to be held against residential mortgage loans than many other types of assets. This type of requirement, along with the more stringent Qualified Thrift Lender test, should increase the incentive for savings and loans to specialize in home-financing activities. Carron and Brumbaugh (1990) find, however, that savings and loans, on average, cannot earn a profit on this type of activity. If so, only the lowest-cost providers of this product can expect to earn a profit.

An Assessment of the FIRREA

The FIRREA will have a major effect on the future of the savings and loan industry as consolidation, restructuring, and shrinkage occur. The resolution of insolvent institutions by the Resolution Trust Corporation should enhance the environment for healthy savings and loans. Deposit rates, for example, should fall as insolvent institutions no longer bid up the cost of funds. Congress and the administration have made the cost of resolving insolvent institutions higher than necessary, however, because, except for an initial $18.8 billion, the least expensive source of funds, Treasury securities, was not tapped so that the cost of the savings and loan debacle could be kept off the federal budget. The complex resolution structure has already caused considerable delay in returning the assets of failed savings and loans to the private sector through intramural squabbling. In addition, its insufficient working capital only compounds the problems of the Resolution Trust Corporation. Worse yet, the $50 billion the FIRREA provided for resolving insolvent institutions was revised sharply upward to a range of $91–139 billion by the administration in the spring of 1990.

A number of FIRREA provisions adversely affect the savings and loan industry more directly. The funding stipulations reduce the earnings of savings and loans and the value of their stock ownership in the FHL banks. Restrictions on asset holdings also reduce earnings. In addition, the affordable housing programs lower the FHL bank earnings that can be passed down to savings and loans, making it harder for savings and loans to meet the higher capital standards.

The more stringent asset restrictions and the more demanding Qualified Thrift Lender test mandate that savings and loans specialize more in home mortgages than many institutions have done over the past decade. These tighter operating constraints impair the ability of savings and loans to diversify and to participate in some potentially profitable activities. The greater enforcement powers given to the Office of Thrift Supervision and the Department of Justice may appear justified in view of egregious excesses by some savings and loan managers and owners. But the threat of substantially increased penalties may have a chilling effect on enterprising savings and loans and those who may wish to disagree with regulatory and supervisory opinions and decisions.

The higher capital requirements should produce a somewhat safer industry. These requirements are inadequate, however, particularly considering the increased competition for financial services and products and the reductions in the value of the savings and loan charter caused by some of the FIRREA-imposed restrictions and by the FIRREA-mandated additional concentration in home mortgages. Furthermore, continuing to rely and act on accounting or book measures of capital rather than on more market-oriented measures results not only in misleading signals to regulators but also in needless costs to some institutions. Higher capital requirements, for example, can be met by selling assets with lower book than market values, such as buildings, core deposits, and selected loans and securities. While sales of these types of assets increase measured capital, they may decrease economic capital as a result of depressed fire-sale prices and taxes paid on capital gains. At the same time, capital-deficient institutions can retain the assets with higher book than market values, such as loans and investment securities with low coupon rates. This particular practice, also employed by troubled institutions in the 1930s and 1940s, has elicited the following comment: "Book valuations tend to distort management's judgement on the advisability of disposing of substandard assets (especially unsold real estate), and frequently the best was sold and the worst held with

96

a consequent increase in the total amount of losses that ultimately had to be accepted" (Lintner 1948, 332).

Unless the federal deposit insurance system is reformed so that owners of savings and loans are required to put much more of their own funds at risk, so that regulators and legislators are prevented from reducing capital requirements when they are most needed, and so that timely and cost-effective actions are taken to reorganize or close inadequately capitalized institutions, a similar debacle may occur.

In sum, the industry will continue to decrease in both number of institutions and assets during the next several years. Shrinkage will result from the resolution of insolvent institutions by the Resolution Trust Corporation, from conversion of savings and loans to commercial bank charters, and from bank holding company acquisitions of savings and loans and savings and loan branches. These changes are encouraged both by the FIRREA and by the significant reduction in the relative value of a savings and loan charter. The remaining savings and loans, however, will appear to operate much like those of the past. As a result of the new Qualified Thrift Lender requirement and other asset restrictions, savings and loans will continue to function primarily as providers of deposit services and home mortgage credit. As table 4–2 shows, those institutions that passed the new capital requirements were as a group more traditional than those savings and loans failing the requirements. This was particularly true of the mutual-type savings and loans. As in the past, however, their poor diversification of both interest rates and credit risk, together with insufficient capital and virtually 100 percent federal deposit insurance, allows the moral hazard problem to persist and could lead to a future disaster. The next chapter discusses how the current structure of the federal deposit insurance system can be reformed. Before moving on, however, we should understand the condition of the savings and loan industry and the actions taken by the Resolution Trust Corporation as the decade of the 1990s began.

A New Decade for Savings and Loans and the Resolution Trust Corporation

During the first quarter of 1990 the savings and loan industry reported losses of $3.4 billion. Of the 2,855 institutions, 2,505 were under the Office of Thrift Supervision and reported losses of $0.3 billion. The remaining 350 institutions, in conservatorship under the supervision of the Resolution Trust Corporation, reported losses of $3.1 billion. The Office of Thrift Supervision categorized the institutions under its purview into four groups: (1) those that are well capitalized and profitable—1,264 institutions with $404 billion in assets; (2) those that meet or are expected to meet the new capital standards—620 institutions with $326 billion in assets; (3) those that are considered troubled because of poor earnings and low capital—311 institutions with $149 billion in assets; and (4) those that are likely to be transferred to the Resolution Trust Corporation—310 institutions with $195 billion in assets. The group 1 institutions had a tangible-capital–to–assets ratio of 6.4 percent and an annualized rate of return on average assets of 0.69 percent. This figure translates into an annualized rate of return on tangible capital of 10.7 percent, which is certainly an unacceptable rate of return over the longer term and therefore underscores the adverse effect that the FIRREA had on the value of the savings and loan charter. The institutions in group 2 earned an annualized rate of return on average assets of only 0.23 percent, with nearly one-fourth reporting losses. Many of these institutions as well as the 621 institutions in groups 3 and 4 that were reporting losses, on average, were likely candidates for the Resolution Trust Corporation. These figures indicate that the savings and loan industry was truly under siege by the FIRREA.

From August 9, 1989, through June 30, 1990, 207 savings and loans with $63 billion in assets were resolved by the Resolution Trust Corporation. The estimated present-value costs for liquidating or selling these institutions was $25 billion, or 40 percent of their assets. Of the total number of resolutions, about half were located in five states—Texas, California, Louisiana, Illinois, and Kansas. Commercial banks insured by the Bank Insurance Fund acquired 131 of the resolved savings and loans, while institutions insured by the Savings Association Insurance Fund acquired 54. The remaining 22 institutions were liquidated. Only 39 percent of the assets in these liquidations and sales, however, were passed to acquirers. Some of these assets, moreover, may be returned to the Resolution Trust Corporation under put-back provisions in the resolution transactions.

The corporation had 247 savings and loans with $128.3 billion in assets in conservatorship and 207 savings and loans with $39.6 billion in assets in receivership under its supervision on June 30, 1990. The corporation's total asset inventory amounted to $168 billion at the end of June, making it the largest "troubled savings and loan" in the history of the world.

From its inception through June 30, 1990, the corporation spent $59.0 billion, including $48.0 billion in outlays for the 207 resolutions and $10.7 billion in advances to savings and loans in conservatorship on June 30 for replacement of high-cost funds and for emergency liquidity purposes. To assist in resolving insolvent institutions, the corporation has borrowed $26.6 billion through the Federal Financing Bank as working capital until the assets acquired have been sold. In accordance with a FIRREA limitation, the corporation's outstanding borrowings and other liabilities cannot exceed the sum of its cash 85 percent of the market value of its other assets, and the remaining borrowing authority of the Resolution Funding Corporation. Clearly, given the poor condition of so many institutions under the Office of Thrift Supervision and the relatively little progress in disposing of assets of insolvent institutions, the corporation is likely to be in business throughout the decade of the 1990s.

5

The Need to Reform
the Insurance System

With the establishment of federal deposit insurance,
the task of preventing banks from developing an unsound or embarrassed condition looms larger than ever
before among the duties of the supervisory and examining authorities. They should, therefore, be given
adequate powers, and be required to make full and effective use of them, in order that an incipient unhealthy
condition may be immediately corrected, and that uneconomic banks may be closed before they reach a state
where liquidation would involve losses. These consid-
erations emphasize the fact that a guaranty-of-deposits
plan is itself no solution of the bank-failure problems
(Bremer 1935, 140).

The events of the 1980s certainly confirm that the mere existence of federal deposit insurance is not a solution to the failure
problems for depository institutions. Indeed, the very availability
of such insurance enabled many inadequately capitalized savings
and loans to engage in high-risk activities and to gamble for resurrection. Insured depositors have no incentive to impose discipline on institutions. Owners too have a diminishing incentive to
impose discipline on the management of their institutions as their
own contributed equity capital is depleted. Once that equity is
fully depleted, the owners have no incentive whatsoever. The only

NOTE: This chapter draws heavily on Barth (May 9–11, 1990) and Barth and
Bartholomew (1990).

100

source of discipline in such a situation remains the regulator and supervisor of the institutions. Yet, during the 1980s, the regulator and supervisor of savings and loans did not "make full and effective use of" their powers "in order that an incipient unhealthy condition" could "be immediately corrected" and "uneconomic" institutions "closed" before they reached "a state" that "would involve losses." The regulator and supervisor, in short, did not reorganize or close inadequately capitalized institutions in a timely manner, with excessive losses being the result. At the time federal deposit insurance was established, however, it was widely recognized and acknowledged that regulation and supervision were supposed to be "a device whereby the government protects a government corporation from undue loss" (Jones 1938, 334).

It should be clear by now that the federal deposit insurance system was the unifying cause of the savings and loan disaster. It should also be clear that the FIRREA did not adequately reform this system to prevent a similar situation from occurring in the future. There remains, therefore, the need to reform the current structure of the nation's federal deposit insurance system. The exact way in which the system should be reformed, however, is quite controversial. Despite this fact, the quotation at the beginning of this chapter is useful in suggesting guidelines for meaningful reform. First, institutions must be required to hold adequate owner-contributed equity capital. Not only does this capital protect against losses, but also it provides owners with an incentive to behave prudently. Second, the capital required to be at risk must be accurately measured. That is, one must determine as precisely as possible the market values of *all* assets and liabilities of an institution. Only in this way can one be sure that capital is truly adequate. Third, undercapitalized institutions must be reorganized or closed before their equity capital has been completely depleted. Only in this way can one be sure that excessive losses will not occur and that taxpayers will therefore be protected as much as possible.

Origins of the Insurance System

The Banking Act of 1933 established the federal deposit insurance system with two plans: a temporary plan that became operative on January 1, 1934, and a permanent plan that was to become operative on July 1, 1934. The temporary plan insured deposits up to $2,500, and the institutions joining the plan were assessed half of 1 percent of the total amount of their insured deposits. Before the operation of the permanent plan, an additional assessment of not more than half of 1 percent was to be levied if the FDIC required additional funds. The permanent plan was to insure deposits in full up to $10,000, 75 percent of the amount between $10,000 and $50,000, and 50 percent of the amount above $50,000. In addition, institutions becoming members in the plan were to be required to subscribe to stock in the FDIC in an amount equal to half of 1 percent of their total deposit liabilities. Half the subscription was due upon joining, while the other half was subject to call by the FDIC. In the event that losses imposed on the FDIC equaled or exceeded one-fourth of 1 percent of the total deposit liabilities of the insured institutions, the institutions were to be assessed one-fourth of 1 percent of their total deposit liabilities. Since this could happen any number of times, there was an *unlimited* liability on the insured institutions for assessments to cover losses. As was noted at the time, "The absence of any such reserve feature renders this a plan of mutual guaranty rather than insurance," a plan that was "attacked vigorously" by the bankers (Emerson 1934, 235).

The permanent plan did not become operative on July 1, 1934. Instead, the temporary plan was extended until the following summer when the Banking Act of 1935 was enacted. The permanent plan was then changed so that the coinsurance element was eliminated, with insurance coverage simply limited to a maximum of $5,000. Furthermore, consistent with the wishes of commercial banks, limits were placed on the assessment powers of the FDIC by eliminating the required stock subscriptions by insured commercial banks and replacing them with an annual assessment rate set at one-twelfth of 1 percent of total deposits. Notably, when this change was being made, some observed that "emphasis has been laid on the necessity of preventing the occurrence of failures" rather than "with providing the wherewithal to protect the depositors of failed banks against losses" (Bremer 1935, 137). But what would happen in the event that losses occurred that exceeded the accumulated assessments levied on insured institutions? Surprisingly, this question was left unanswered. No specific mechanism was therefore explicitly put into place that would allocate *all* losses resulting from failures in a predetermined way among the insured institutions and the taxpayers.

The assessment rate levied upon commercial banks was arrived at as follows. From July 1, 1864, the beginning of the national banking system, to June 30, 1934, about 16,000 commercial banks suspended operations. Losses to the depositors in these commercial banks were estimated at $3 billion, or thirty-three cents per $100 of total deposits, with twenty-one cents being lost at national banks and forty-two cents at state banks. The experience over this seventy-year period, therefore, indicated that to cover losses by all depositors in the suspended commercial banks, the assessment rate would have had to be set at one-third of 1 percent of total deposits. Excluding the losses incurred during the three depression periods—1873–1878, 1892–1897, and 1931–1934—reduced the assessment rate to one-eighth of 1 percent. Before the final permanent plan was completed, the FDIC stated that "to ask the banks to bear the entire cost of insurance at a rate comparable to the experience of losses over the past 70 years would subject them to a heavy burden at the present time" (Crowley 1935, 11). More specifically,

> We arrived at the one-twelfth of 1 percent in this way: we do not believe that one-twelfth of 1 percent will build large enough reserves for the Deposit Insurance Corporation for the future, but the earning capacity of the banks right now is very low. We are interested, first, in the banks having sufficient income themselves so that they may take their losses currently and so that they may build reserves for the future. This is the greatest protection to the Deposit Insurance Corporation (Crowley 1935, 48).

The assessment rate, therefore, was never set high enough to reflect historical losses for commercial banks. Once again quoting from the FDIC, "The raising of a sufficient revenue, solely through the levying of premiums against the deposits of those receiving direct insurance benefits will not be a fair distribution of the burden." The reason for this view was that "banking is no longer merely a private business proposition. It involves great social consequences. The stability of the banking system affects the economic prosperity of the country." Of course, while "the banks must pay a fair share of this income, . . . a contribution from other sources to help build . . . [the banks'] reserves might be considered" (Crowley 1935, 10 and 49). In the case of the present savings and loan troubles, a contribution was indeed made from sources outside the industry, but that contribution—from taxpayers—was made only after the problems had occurred, not before. Had the contribution been made before the disaster and not after, it could have been significantly smaller.

The history of the premiums and coverage for federally insured deposits at both savings and loans and commercial banks is presented in appendix F. The trend has certainly been to broaden the insurance coverage while simultaneously reducing the insurance premium. Furthermore, regarding savings and loans, the National Housing Act "states that no member can receive more than" the stated coverage limit "in any one S&L, no matter how many accounts he holds." "Congress," however, "then said that a member could be a corporation, partnership, or association, as well as an individual person." Things did not stop here, because "the S&L and FHLBB lawyers started providing their own definitions." Subsequently, "each different joint account received separate insurance," and "the National Housing Act was amended to provide that each trust estate was separately insured." To control "the virtually unlimited coverage that had evolved during the 1950's," the FHLBB issued a regulation regarding coverage in July 1967. This regulation, however, "is very inadequate" because "both its wording and the concepts involved are so intricate that only lawyers can follow them—and then only after a great deal of study" (Marvell 1969, 106–9). More recently, in the early 1980s, the FHLBB broadened the insurance coverage:

> Recognizing that an important element in restoring the health of thrifts is improving their ability to compete for new capital, the Bank Board, through opinions issued by the Office of the General Counsel and amendments to the regulations, also broadened insurance coverage for a variety of accounts. Insurance coverage was extended to cover beneficiaries of pension plans as well as other trusteed employee benefit plans, certificates of deposits held by a trustee as security for holders of tax-exempt bonds and holders of participation interests in certificates of deposit held by broker-dealers (*Annual Report*, 1982, Federal Home Loan Bank Board, April 1983, 15).

The situation is even worse for commercial banks because of the

104

"too-big-to-fail" doctrine, according to which the adverse consequences of a big bank's failure—or, more accurately, depositor payoff—are so severe that such an act cannot be permitted to occur. Such a doctrine argues for 100 percent deposit guarantees. To the extent that some banks are indeed considered too big to fail, not only are smaller institutions put at a competitive disadvantage but also whatever market discipline exists is seriously weakened (see Haraf 1990).

Issues in Reforming the Insurance System

The federal government's appropriate role with respect to depository institutions is to make available accurate financial information, to be able and willing to act on such information, and to decide who shares, and to what extent, in the losses resulting from insolvencies. The primary rationale for federal deposit insurance is that without it depositors might engage in widespread runs on depository institutions, even solvent institutions, and thereby disrupt the payments system and the credit process. As a result, not only would insolvent institutions lose, but also solvent institutions might be driven into insolvency as they were forced to sell assets at fire-sale prices to meet the heavy deposit withdrawals. Without federal deposit insurance, of course, the losses would be shared by the owners of equity-contributed capital and depositors, not taxpayers. The fundamental problem with depository institutions that earn profits by transforming liquid assets into illiquid assets is, therefore, that inadequate information prevents depositors from distinguishing the solvent from the insolvent institutions. More broadly, if a situation led to a widespread run on the nation's depository institutions, everybody in the entire economy would be seriously and adversely affected.

A lender-of-last-resort, however, could supply liquidity to those institutions that are solvent but still incurring heavy deposit withdrawals. If this were done, only the insolvent institutions would be forced to close by the heavy withdrawal of deposits. Yet, for the lender-of-last-resort to function properly, it, like a federal insurer, must have sufficient information to distinguish between solvent and insolvent banks and then the ability and willingness to act. "In any event," one observer remarked, "the period from 1929 through the banking holiday of 1933 demonstrated that the lender-of-last-resort mechanism, by itself, is insufficient to guarantee stability of the overall banking system"

(Working Group of the Cabinet Council on Economic Affairs 1985, 2).

The major benefit of federal deposit insurance is that it removes the incentive for depositors to run on depository institutions, both solvent and insolvent. Such a system therefore prevents runs and protects small depositors but simultaneously exposes taxpayers to losses. The necessary condition for protecting taxpayers is for the federal insurer to reorganize or close inadequately capitalized institutions quickly and cost effectively. Otherwise, the losses from any resulting insolvencies will necessarily be excessive and potentially large enough to be borne, at least partly, by taxpayers. Although certainly necessary, early reorganization or closure may not be sufficient to protect taxpayers. The FDIC recognized and acknowledged, when federal deposit insurance was established in the 1930s, that the premium structure would *not* "build large enough reserves . . . for the future." But it was decided at the time that such a structure was preferable to imposing unlimited liability upon the insured institutions for assessments to cover any and all losses. Yet, even in the case of unlimited liability, the funds available to cover losses would presumably be limited to the total owner-contributed equity capital for all insured institutions. (As a historical aside, "Previous to July 1, 1937, bank creditors were protected against asset depreciation to an extent considerably greater than that indicated by the capital ratio figures by double liability" [Jones 1938, 337].) In a world of uncertainty, events could unfold that would so depress asset values that the combined equity capital of all institutions would be wiped out. After all, this was the case for the savings and loan industry in the late 1970s and the early 1980s. Taxpayers, then, can never be completely protected against loss so long as federal deposit insurance exists.

Properly structuring federal deposit insurance is a balancing act. The major goals are to prevent widespread runs and to protect taxpayers as much as possible. To prevent runs, one must guarantee depositors against loss while exposing taxpayers to potential losses. These losses are most likely to result from highly risky activities induced by deposit insurance and from non–cost-effective actions of the federal insurer to resolve troubled institutions. Information is crucial in this balancing act. *If* one could assess the market value of all the assets and liabilities of an institution, then whether that institution were solvent or adequately capitalized could be determined. To reduce taxpayers' exposure to insolvency losses, one would simply assess the market value of an institution and then close it when the market value of owner-contributed equity reached zero.

Market values, however, are not readily available for all assets and liabilities of insured institutions. One must therefore rely upon estimates of "true" market values by comparing values for assets and liabilities currently in the marketplace with those that are at insured institutions. Questions arise, however, about whether the estimates reflect liquidation values or going-concern values when applied to an entire institution. One may also rely on the market value of the equity capital issued by stock-type institutions. Not all these institutions issue actively traded stock, however. Furthermore, even for those institutions whose stock is actively traded, the values will necessarily incorporate the value of federal deposit insurance to the institutions (see Merton 1980 and 1977; Brumbaugh and Hemel 1984; Ronn and Verma 1986; and Barth, Page, and Brumbaugh 1990). In the case of savings and loans, moreover, there are many mutual-type institutions. Despite these difficulties, and as formidable as they may be, more reliance can and should be placed on market-oriented measures of the financial condition of insured institutions, because, as Edward Kane (*The S&L Insurance Mess*, 1989) states, "The keystone of effective reform is developing a clean windshield" (p.168).

The government must require insured depository institutions to hold "adequate" capital relative to their assets, because capital provides not only the first line of defense in the protection of taxpayers but also the necessary incentive for institutions to engage in prudent behavior. Clearly, those institutions operating with inadequate capital and retaining access to federal deposit insurance are most likely to undertake the riskiest activities. The government should therefore set reasonably high capital requirements, collect the best available market-value information to properly measure capital, and then reorganize or close institutions when their owner-contributed equity capital has been seriously dissipated or depleted (see Brookings Institution 1989). None of these actions, however, was taken by the government during the savings and loan crisis of the 1980s, especially the early 1980s, or even, for that matter, during the 1960s and the 1970s when the savings and loan industry also encountered significant difficulties.

The assessed deposit insurance premiums should reflect the

fair value of the deposit insurance to an institution. The riskier the activities of an insured institution and the weaker its capital position, the greater the value deposit insurance will be to that institution and therefore the higher the premium should be. But simply adjusting deposit premiums upward to eliminate the subsidy cannot substitute for the early intervention into the affairs of an institution whose owner-contributed equity is being depleted. Indeed, for the better protection of taxpayers, it may make sense to reexamine the original insurance plan in which insured institutions had to subscribe to stock on an unlimited basis in an attempt to ensure the solvency of the insurance fund.

Proposals for Reform

One proposal to reform the federal deposit insurance system would simply require that all insured deposits be backed or collateralized by highly liquid and thus essentially riskless assets. This approach would protect the payments system from widespread runs because depositors would know that the market value of the assets would—apart from relatively minor fluctuations, fraud, and insider abuse—equal the value of the insured deposits. This limitation on allowable assets would convert the current commercial bank into a "narrow bank"—the narrowness of the bank depending on the assets allowed to be purchased with insured deposits, which in turn depends on the availability and liquidity of specific assets. Under this proposal, all remaining assets would be put into a separate entity funded solely with uninsured liabilities and owner-contributed equity capital.

The narrow bank proposal accomplishes several goals. First, it protects small depositors. Second, it prevents widespread runs by using only insured deposits to acquire those assets whose market value equals the amount of deposits. Third, it protects taxpayers from losses because declines in asset values are essentially eliminated. Although the narrow or payments portion of the institution is fully protected against loss, the remaining or credit portion is not. Any losses associated with the credit portion, however, are borne by the owners of the uninsured liabilities and capital, not taxpayers. Fourth, if implemented, the proposal actually makes deposit insurance redundant and the need for the extensive regulation and supervision of depository institutions relatively unimportant.

108

Although the narrow bank proposal has many desirable features, a concern is that it eliminates the *raison d'etre* of depository institutions, which is the conversion of liquid liabilities into illiquid assets. By narrowing the range of assets available to these institutions to highly liquid assets alone, will not the profits be squeezed out? In any event, this intriguing proposal has been most recently advocated by Robert E. Litan (1987). A more extreme version of this proposal was advocated during congressional hearings on the Banking Act of 1935. As Robert H. Hemphill, a former officer of the Federal Reserve System, stated at those hearings, "I thought reserves should be progressively increased until every bank could pay any part of its checking accounts—demand deposits—at any time. Until this was done I considered banking a gamble with the public always loser" (Hemphill 1935, 501). Irving Fisher of Yale University also testified at the hearings. It was his view that for every dollar subject to check one should have an equal amount of "Federal Reserve or Government credit which can be turned into money" (Fisher 1935, 542). As a result, "Anybody knowing that he could get 100 cents on the dollar, no matter if every other depositor demands his, at the same time would not demand much, if any" (Fisher 1935, 445). Furthermore, he went on to say, "There would then be no need for many, if any, banking laws" (Fisher 1935, 542). Interestingly, another Yale University professor, James Tobin, 1981 Nobel Prize winner for economics, stated just over a half-century later that one should "require all federally insured deposits to be backed 100% by safe liquid assets—specifically, for example, by currency, balances at Federal Reserve banks, and U.S. Treasury or federally guaranteed obligations not longer than five years" (Tobin 1989).

Another proposal is to retain the broader depository institutions and federal deposit insurance but to impose more market discipline. This could be accomplished through coinsurance—as was originally enacted during the 1930s—or by reducing the amount of deposit insurance coverage, either per account or per depositor. The rationale is that by exposing depositors to more risk, they will demand higher interest rates on the funds that are placed at institutions engaged in relatively risky activities and with relatively little owner-contributed equity capital. This imposes discipline on institutions operating in a competitive market. The federal insurer can monitor the rates paid on uninsured deposits, moreover, to enable it to assess better the financial condition of an institution. Such a proposal certainly exposes the taxpayer to less risk, but it also increases the risk of a widespread run in comparison with the current federal insurance system.

Still another proposal for reform that imposes market discipline is the proposal for mutual- or cross-guarantees by the depository institutions themselves (see Ely 1985 and 1989). Institutions would establish a fairly elaborate system under which the entire capital of the industry would be available to cover any losses resulting from insolvencies. By charging appropriate risk-sensitive premiums to one another, the institutions themselves would provide the mechanism to induce individual savings and loans to control their exposure to risk. In the event that abnormal or catastrophic losses occur, the federal government or taxpayers would serve as a backstop to the depository institutions. There are at least three potential limitations to this proposal. First, depositors may engage in widespread runs for fear that the combined capital of the insured institutions is insufficient to protect them. Second, the institutions themselves have an incentive to overstate any losses—the opposite of the incentive that inadequately capitalized savings and loans had during the early and middle 1980s—to protect their capital from being used to cover losses and thus to pressure the federal government to step forward prematurely and share in those losses. Third, how the proposal will ensure that inadequately capitalized institutions will be reorganized or closed quickly and cost effectively is not clear.

To the extent the federal government will always be involved, perhaps its role should be defined more clearly, thus making that role more susceptible to public scrutiny. Institutions could rely on a form of reinsurance in which the federal insurer would assume some relatively high percentage of all losses from insolvencies of depository institutions and the reinsurer the remaining percentage. The reinsurer would be responsible for assessing the riskiness of a depository institution and for determining an appropriate insurance premium. The federal insurer could then, if it wished, apply this premium to all insured deposits. The merit of this particular proposal is that market discipline would be imposed as specialized private firms analyze the financial condition of insured depository institutions. By putting their own capital at risk, these firms would have every incentive to collect and assess the best information by which to set a deposit insurance premium. More generally, such firms would establish contractual relationships with depository institutions to provide market-based information to the federal insurer and the public that could lead to the reorganization or closure of inadequately capitalized institutions more quickly and cost effectively.

The entire issue of private insurance for depository institutions was discussed in a seminal paper written almost twenty years ago. As Kenneth Scott and Thomas Mayer stated at the time:

> This [private insurance] is probably the most promising solution. Part, if not all, of the pricing judgment could be transferred to the private sector—for example, by having the federal insurance corporations cover less than 100 percent of the risk and requiring the insured bank or S&L to obtain some portion (for example, the first $X million) of its coverage from private sources. The resulting demand would bring a new form of private insurance into existence and thereby create a large, independent set of risk judgments. Conceivably, one could go further and require all institutions to obtain private insurance, limiting the federal role either to reinsurance or to separate coverage of the fourth category of failure (Scott and Mayer 1971, 575).

In sum, all proposals for restructuring the federal deposit insurance system involve producing and monitoring accurate information, stipulating adequate owner-contributed equity capital, and reorganizing or closing undercapitalized depository institutions cost effectively. If one cannot obtain good information for a broad range of assets or if inadequately capitalized institutions cannot be reorganized or closed efficiently, the narrow bank proposal or a modification thereof is quite attractive. If one can obtain enough information on which to set appropriate insurance premiums and those firms both paying and receiving the premiums can earn an acceptable profit, then the government and private firms, either independently or cooperatively, can operate an insurance plan. If the government cannot act appropriately on the available information, then heavy, if not exclusive, private sector involvement is desirable. If private sector capital is insufficient to prevent widespread runs, heavy, if not exclusive, federal sector involvement is desirable.

The basic question is, Who can produce and monitor the

111

best information to determine with reasonable accuracy the financial condition of depository institutions? The depositors may not thus engage in widespread runs on *all* depository institutions. This problem is solved with the narrow bank because depositors would have enough information so that any losses would be so low that they would not run. Federal deposit insurance also provides depositors with sufficient information about the safety and security of their deposits so that they will not run. But the government may inadequately protect taxpayers by either failing to produce and monitor information accurate enough to determine the financial condition of depository institutions or not acting upon such information quickly and cost effectively. In such a situation, the private sector can assist the government by producing and monitoring accurate information and then setting deposit insurance premiums that reflect the riskiness of the activities of the depository institutions, taking into account the owner-contributed equity capital. By putting its own capital at risk, the private sector has every incentive to set the premiums appropriately. More generally, do private insurance firms, including the depository institutions, act either as reinsurers or as self-insurers so that a small portion or even all of the losses are borne by these firms? In the case of self-insurance, does the federal government act as a backstop against catastrophic losses? To the extent that the federal government will always be in the picture, it may make sense to investigate the reinsurer proposal more closely (see, however, Gorton 1985 and Calomiris 1989). The role of the federal government would then be better defined and thus susceptible to greater public scrutiny. Besides, the federal government is the ultimate reinsurer.

The Bottom Line to Reforming
Federal Deposit Insurance

The savings and loan problems have revealed fundamental weaknesses in the current structure of the federal deposit insurance system. As a result, recognition and acknowledgment that this system needs reform are growing. While all the reform proposals discussed here merit serious attention and discussion, a broader issue must not be overlooked: the ultimate protection to taxpayers is profitable and well-capitalized depository institutions. To be profitable and well capitalized, depository institutions must op-

112

erate in a healthy and prosperous economy. One cannot therefore focus solely or exclusively on the structure of the federal deposit insurance system but instead should seek ways to improve the profitability and capitalization of these institutions. Unless they can earn adequate profits over time to generate the retained earnings to build up capital or to pay the dividends to attract additional outside capital, they will never have enough capital to protect taxpayers. After all, the reserves to cover losses in the federal deposit insurance system come directly from the profits and capital of the insured institutions. This means that any *serious* proposal for reforming the insurance system must specify the regulatory and supervisory structure in which depository institutions will operate. This structure directly affects the profits and capital of institutions, as was so vividly demonstrated by savings and loans in the 1980s. If narrow banks are created but cannot earn adequate profits, how can taxpayers be protected? If depository institutions cannot earn adequate profits given the current regulatory and supervisory structure, how can cross-guarantees or self-insurance protect taxpayers?

The answer to these questions is quite obviously that taxpayers can be protected only if the depository institutions are profitable and well capitalized. But what if the regulatory and supervisory structure prevents these institutions from adapting to changing market forces and thereby adversely affects their profits and capitalization? The reform of federal deposit insurance per se cannot solve this problem. Instead, regulatory and supervisory reform must be integral to deposit insurance reform. A major lesson from the current savings and loan problems is that the regulatory and supervisory structure can inhibit and even prevent institutions from adapting to changing market forces, so that they become insufficiently profitable and inadequately capitalized given the risk to which the liability holders are exposed. In such a situation, virtually all the risk is simply shifted to the government. At the same time, those financial firms that compete in a less regulated and supervised environment only worsen the situation for the insured depository institutions, since those firms can easily and rapidly respond to market forces.

In sum, an efficient financial services industry requires that firms be allowed to adapt to changing conditions. The way to be sure such adaptation does indeed generate efficiency gains is through competition in the marketplace. One must be careful, however, to prevent competition from being socially destructive by imposing excessive insolvency losses upon taxpayers because some firms operate with subsidized federally insured deposits. The value of federally insured deposits to well-capitalized—that is, with owner-contributed equity capital—firms, however, is near zero. The reform of the current structure of the federal insurance system and the regulatory and supervisory system, therefore, must create a profitable, well-capitalized, and competitive financial services industry. This outcome is important for savings and loans and commercial banks, which together have experienced a significant decline in their share of total assets held by all financial service firms as other relatively new, uninsured, and less-regulated financial firms have become increasingly important. It is time to eliminate many, if not all, of the geographical, product, ownership, and activity restrictions on these insured depository institutions by the McFadden Act, the Bank Holding Company Act, the FIRREA, the Glass-Steagall Act, and other federal and state laws and regulations. Such restrictions effectively induce commerce to create its own financial infrastructure and thereby weaken the profitability and capitalization of the insured depository institutions. As a result, the value of the federal insurance to the institutions increases as does the risk exposure of taxpayers.

It is time to reverse the decline in profitability and capitalization for savings and loans and commercial banks. While such a reversal requires reform in the regulatory and supervisory system, it must not increase the risk exposure of taxpayers. The federal deposit insurance system must therefore be reformed as well: insured depository institutions have to be allowed to engage in a wide range of activities and to be owned by a wide range of firms subject to appropriate capital standards, monitoring systems, and early intervention devices. Whether a universal bank or a new holding company structure would be most appropriate in such a reformed system must be carefully examined. Whether only one agency should charter and another agency should insure the depository institutions must also be carefully examined (see Breeden 1990, for a discussion of these issues). Certainly the restructuring that has occurred in the industry in recent years has been accompanied by both shrinkage and consolidation.

6
Lessons for the 1990s and Beyond

The savings and loan industry has undergone tremendous change since the first institutions were established in 1831. During most of the ensuing years, savings and loans specialized in gathering savings and then using them to finance home ownership. The activity remained relatively profitable for many years, since very little competition came from other financial service firms. Before World War II, the savings and loan industry had experienced only two periods of major problems: the economic downturn in the 1890s and the severe depression in the 1930s. Neither of these adverse periods, however, revealed any fundamental weaknesses in the institutional design of savings and loans. Not surprisingly, therefore, the industry bounced back from its problems fairly quickly.

After World War II, the marketplace began to change as inflation accelerated and interest rates moved upward. By the late 1970s and the early 1980s not only had interest rates reached double-digit levels but also they had become quite volatile. The changing economic environment was accompanied by new and sweeping innovations in the informational technology that permitted tremendous efficiencies in the production and monitoring of information. As a result, new products were developed and marketed by financial service firms. Mainly because of government regulations and supervision, the nation's depository institutions were unable to adapt to the changing marketplace, which created an opening for new types of financial service firms as well as opportunities for other firms to expand their range of financial services. All these events became quite clear when the savings

115

and loan industry suffered the third and worst period in its entire 150-year history: the 1980s were devastating for savings and loans and for the first time their flawed institutional design was openly revealed. Although federal deposit insurance could prevent runs and protect small depositors, it needed to be reformed to protect taxpayers. It also became clear that government regulation and supervision could increase the riskiness of federally insured depository institutions. By permitting institutions to operate with inadequate capital, the federal insurance system was subsidizing such institutions while simultaneously increasing the risk to the taxpayers. For the better protection of taxpayers, institutions operating with federally insured deposits must be adequately capitalized. Reforming the insurance system by requiring adequate capital (which means being able to measure accurately all assets and liabilities) and by requiring that inadequately capitalized institutions be reorganized or closed is, however, the most appropriate way to protect taxpayers better. To achieve adequate capitalization, though, federally insured depository institutions must be profitable so as to build up their capital through retained earnings or the issuance of stock. In a changing marketplace, the depository institutions need the flexibility to adapt by offering new products. Otherwise, they will not remain competitive and hence profitable. It is therefore essential to reexamine the entire regulatory and supervisory apparatus that was established along with federal deposit insurance in the 1930s. Most of the ownership and activity restrictions inhibit and prevent adaptation to changing market forces. Although the government can prevent institutions from adapting, it cannot prevent the marketplace from changing, and therein lies the real problem.

The main lesson to be learned from the great savings and loan debacle is that institutions must be able to respond to changing market forces through an evolving institutional design. At the same time, if they operate with federally insured deposits, they must always be adequately capitalized. It is owner-contributed equity capital, not activity and ownership restrictions, that ultimately protects taxpayers.

Appendixes

APPENDIX A: EVOLUTION OF FEDERAL SAVINGS AND LOAN POWERS, 1933–1982

	Home Mortgages	Nonresidential Mortgages	Land Development	Direct Investments	Service Corporations	Construction Loans	Corporate Bonds	Education Loans	Consumer Loans	Commercial Loans	Leasing of Personal Property	Investment in Comm'l Paper	Credit Cards
Home Owners' Loan Act, 1933 (enacted)	Yes ($20,000 loan limit)	Yes (15% of assets)											
Housing Act of 1959, 1959 (enacted)			Yes (loans up to 5% of assets)										
Housing Act of 1961, 1961 (enacted)				Yes (5% of assets in bus. dev. corp)									
Public law 87-779, 1962 (enacted)		Yes (20% of assets)											
Public law 88-560, 1964 (enacted)				Yes (2% of assets in urb. renew. area)	Yes (1% of assets)								

(Appendix A continues)

119

	Home Mortgages	Nonresidential Mortgages	Land Development	Direct Investments	Service Corporations	Construction Loans	Corporate Bonds	Education Loans	Consumer Loans	Commercial Loans	Leasing of Personal Property	Investment in Comm'l Paper	Credit Cards
Administration's fed. savings bank bill, 1965[a] (proposed)	Yes ($35,000 or 2% of assets[a])	Yes	Yes (loans)	Yes (up to 50% of capital)	Yes (no limit)		Yes	Yes (up to 5% of assets)	Yes (up to $5,000)				
Hunt commission study,[b] 1972 (proposed)	Yes (statutory loan limit dele.)	Yes	Yes	Yes (up to 3% assets)		Yes	Yes	Yes (up to 3% of assets)	Yes (up to 10% of assets)	Yes (up to 3% of assets)		Yes (up to 3% of assets)	Yes
Administration's proposed "financial constitutions act" 1973[c] (proposed)		Yes		Yes (for community development)		Yes	Yes (up to 10% of assets)		Yes (up to 10% of assets)			Yes (up to 10% of assets)	Yes
"Fine Study" legislation passed senate, 1975[d] (proposed)	Yes (statutory loan limit dele.)	Yes (30% of assets)	Yes (loans)	Yes (for community development)	Yes (1% of assets)	Yes	Yes	Yes (30% of assets)	Yes (30% of assets)			Yes (30% of assets)	Yes
House banking committee print, 1976[e] (proposed)	Yes (statutory loan limit dele.)	Yes (20% of assets)		Yes (for community development)	Yes (1% of assets)	Yes (20% of assets)	Yes	Yes (20% of assets)	Yes (20% of assets)			Yes	

Public law 95-630 (1978) (enacted)	Yes ($60,000 loan limit[h])	Yes (20% of assets)	Yes (5% of assets)	Yes (2% assets for community dev.)	Yes (1% of assets)	Yes (5% of assets)	Yes (5% of assets)		Yes (10% of assets)	Yes (20% of assets)	Yes / Yes
Administration proposal 1979[f] (proposed)								Yes (10% of assets)	Yes (10% of assets)	Yes (20% of assets)	Yes / Yes
Depository institutions deregulation act 1980 (enacted)	Yes (90% loan-to-value limit)	Yes (20% of assets)		Yes (2% of assets for community dev.; 5% bus. dev.)	Yes (3% of assets)	Yes (5% of assets)	Yes (20% of assets)	Yes (5% of assets)	Yes (20% of assets)	Yes (20% of assets)	Yes
Administration proposal 1981[k] (proposed)	Yes (statutory loan-to-value limit dele.)	Yes (no limit)		Yes (in small bus. invest. comps.)	Yes (5% of assets)		Yes (no limit)	Yes (no limit)	Yes (no limit)	Yes (no limit)	Yes (10% of assets)
Garn-St Germain 1982 (enacted)	Yes (statutory loan-to-value limit dele.)	Yes (40% of assets)		Yes (1% of assets in small bus. inv. comps.)			Yes[k]	Yes (30% of assets)	Yes[l] (10% of assets)	Yes (10% of assets)	

(Appendix A continues)

APPENDIX A (continued)

	Home Mortgages	Nonresidential Mortgages	Land Development	Direct Investments	Service Corporations	Construction Loans	Corporate Bonds	Education Loans	Consumer Loans	Commercial Loans	Leasing of Personal Property	Investment in Comm'l Paper	Credit Cards
Year first authorized	1933	1933	1959	1961	1964	1978	1980	1978	1980	1982	1982	1980	1980

a. H.R. 14 and H.R. 11506, 89th Cong.

b. Report, Pres. Comm. on Fin. Structure and Reg. (1972)

c. S. 2591, 93rd Cong. (1973)

d. S. 1267, 94th Cong. (1975)

e. Financial Reform Act of 1976, 94th Cong. (1976)

f. Depos. Inst. Dereg. Act, 96th Cong. (1979)

g. S. 1703, 97th Cong. (1981).

h. The bill also provided an 80% loan-to-value limit that could be waived by reg.

i. The limit was raised to $75,000 in 1979, Public Law 96-161.

j. By regulation, up to 1% in unrated bonds.

k. While the Garn-St Germain Act continues the placement of corp. bond investments in the 20% of assets basket, the Bank Board interpreted the Act to permit up to 100% of assets in corporate bonds, with up to 1% in unrated bonds.

l. By regulation, the Bank Board interpreted this authority to include investment in unrated corp. bonds up to 10% of assets.

SOURCE: Raymond Natter, "Deregulation of Federal Savings Associations 1961 through 1982," undated mimeo.

APPENDIX B:

*Depository Institutions Deregulation and Monetary Control Act,
March 1980*

- Phased out Regulation Q over a six-year period ending on March 31, 1986

- Increased federal insurance of accounts from $40,000 to $100,000

- Authorized NOW accounts for individuals and not-for-profit organizations at all federally insured depositories as of December 31, 1980

- Authorized federally chartered savings and loans to offer credit card services and to exercise trust and fiduciary powers

- Authorized federal savings and loans to invest up to 20 percent of their assets in a combination of consumer loans, commercial paper, and corporate debt securities, and to invest up to 3 percent of their assets in service corporations, provided that one-half of the investment exceeding 1 percent is allocated to investments that serve primarily community or inner-city development purposes

- Expanded the authority of federal savings and loans to make real estate loans by removing geographical lending restrictions; provided for a 90 percent loan-to-value limit in place of the previous $75,000 limit; removed the first-lien restriction on residential real estate loans

- Expanded the authority of federal savings and loans to make acquisition, development, and construction loans

- Preempted state usury ceilings for residential real estate and certain other loans

- Authorized savings and loans to issue mutual capital certificates to be included in the general reserve and net worth of the issuing institution

(Appendix B continues)

Garn-St Germain Depository Institutions Act, December 1982

- Provided for broader capital assistance programs

- Expanded the powers of federal insurers in dealing with troubled institutions

- Required the Depository Institutions Deregulation Committee to create a deposit account that would be competitive with money market mutual funds

- Preempted state laws that restricted the enforcement of due-on-sale clauses

- Permitted federal institutions to accept demand accounts in connection with a business relationship

- Expanded considerably the asset powers of federal institutions, including increasing the statutory limit on commercial mortgage loans and consumer loans to 40 percent and 30 percent of assets, respectively; permitted commercial loans and leases to 10 percent of assets each

Tax Reform Act, October 1986

- Reduced the deductible contribution to bad debt reserves to 8 percent of taxable income (down from 40 percent)

- Replaced the minimum corporate tax

- Lowered the corporate tax rate so that the maximum rate would be 34 percent (down from 46 percent)

- Included special rules governing the carryover of net operating losses of a troubled savings and loan by its acquirer

- Reduced the depreciation benefits of commercial and residential property

- Limited the offsetting losses on passive investments that affect limited partnership syndications and eliminated favorable capital gains treatment

- Provided for 3-year carrybacks and 15-year carryforwards for savings and loan net operating losses

Competitive Equality Banking Act, August 1987

- Provided a funding plan to assist the FSLIC. Under this plan, the bank board is to charter a Financing Corporation (FICO) that would be authorized to borrow up to $10.825 billion (no more than $3.75 billion per year) by issuing long-term bonds to the public. The FICO is to place the funds it raises with the FSLIC in exchange for nonvoting capital stock and capital certificates. The FICO would be capitalized with the retained earnings of the FHI banks. Most of these earnings will be invested in deep-discount government bonds that at maturity would provide for the repayment of the principal of the FICO's bonds. Interest payments on the FICO's bonds would be met from insurance premiums assessed on FSLIC-insured thrift institutions.

- Blocked any savings and loan institution from leaving the FSLIC for one year. After one year, any institution that exits the fund is to be charged an exit fee of $5/6$ of 1 percent of total deposits.

- Provided for the phase out of the FSLIC special assessment, unless the FHLBB determines that extreme pressure continues to exist

- Mandated the FHLBB to prescribe capital recovery regulations (forbearance provisions) for troubled but well-managed and viable institutions in a manner that will maximize the long-term viability of the thrift industry at the lowest cost to the FSLIC; provided forbearance to institutions with capital of $1/2$ percent or more, provided that their problems are caused by economic adversity beyond their control

- Required that a new appraisal standard for real estate be established that is consistent with the practices of the federal banking agencies

- Required all ARMs on one- to four-family dwelling units to include an interest rate cap

(Appendix B continues)

- Established a new qualified thrift lender test that requires that an insured institution must maintain 60 percent of its tangible assets in housing and housing-related investments for the institution to have Qualified Thrift Lender status

- Reduced the eligibility for FHL bank advances for institutions that do not have Qualified Thrift Lender status

- Provided that the current exemption from the nonthrift activity restrictions for unitary savings and loan holding companies is available to acquiring firms only when the subsidiary savings and loan has Qualified Thrift Lender status

SOURCE: Barth and Bradley (1989).

APPENDIX C:

Important Regulatory Developments in the Savings and Loan Industry in the 1980s

Item and Date	Key Provisions
Borrowing limitations (May 1980)	Liberalized and simplified limitations on borrowing by federal savings and loans and FSLIC-insured institutions; permitted FSLIC members to borrow up to 50 percent of assets (was 50 percent of savings) and increased the limit on borrowing outside of the FHL Bank System to 20 percent of assets (was 10 percent)
Real estate lending (November 1980)	Permitted loans secured by one- to four-family properties in excess of 90 percent of value; permitted federal institutions to make real estate and property improvement loans without dollar limit (except on borrower); removed the requirement of having the first lien on mortgage loans
Borrowing limitations (February 1981)	Liberalized limitations and increased the ability of institutions to borrow without prior notice or prior approval; permitted FSLIC-insured institutions to borrow from sources outside the FHL Bank System under much more liberal rules than formerly
Adjustable-rate mortgages (April 1981)	Authorized federal savings and loans to make, purchase, participate in, and otherwise deal in adjustable-rate mortgages; required that adjustments to the interest rate be based upon the movement of an index agreed to by the lender and borrower; preempted state laws that would restrict federal savings and loans from making adjustable-rate mortgage loans; superseded the variable-rate mort-

(Appendix C continues)

Item and Date	*Key Provisions*
	gage regulation of 1979 and the renegotiable-rate mortgage regulation of 1980. These earlier regulations provided for very constrained types of adjustable mortgage loans, especially concerning the indexes that could be used and the amount that interest rates could be changed.
Service corporations (May 1981)	Expanded the list of activities in which service corporations of federal institutions may engage without prior bank board approval and liberalized restrictions on customers to whom service corporations may provide services
Futures transactions (July 1981)	Eliminated eligibility requirements and expanded the ability of FSLIC-insured institutions to participate in the futures markets, including permitting the use of any futures contract designated by the Commodities Futures Trading Commission and based upon a security in which the institution has authority to invest
FHL bank advances (August 1981)	Increased the amount that FHL bank members may borrow from their district bank up to the lesser of their legal maximum borrowing limit or 50 percent of their assets
Borrowing limitations (January 1982)	Permitted FSLIC-insured institutions to borrow outside the FHL bank system without limit and to sell loans with recourse, subject to certain rules
Financial options (August 1982)	Permitted FSLIC-insured institutions to buy financial options, to write call options without position limits, and to write put options subject to limits

APPENDIX C (continued)

Item and Date	Key Provisions
Special assessment (November 1982)	FHLBB issued an advance notice of proposed rule making on a plan to increase the total level of premium collections.
Junk bonds (May 1983)	Categorized corporate debt securities as commercial lending. Therefore, federal associations were permitted to invest up to 10 percent of assets in junk bonds through their commercial lending authority and an additional 1 percent through their explicit authority to hold corporate debt securities.
Loan-to-value ratios (May 1983)	Eliminated specific loan-to-value ratios for various types of secured loans
FHL bank advances (September 1983)	Permitted FHL banks to make advances for terms up to 10 years (was 10 years)
Brokered deposits (April 1984)	Joint regulation with FDIC limited the insurance coverage afforded to deposits placed with insured institutions by brokers, with certain specified exceptions
Brokered deposits (June 1984)	Judge Gesell of the U.S. District Court enjoined the implementation of the April 1984 brokered deposits regulation stating that the insurers had exceeded their statutory limits
Interest-rate-risk management (July 1984)	Required that the board of directors of FSLIC-insured institutions develop, adopt, implement, and periodically adjust policy and procedures for interest-rate-risk management.
Finance subsidiaries (July 1984)	Permitted federal institutions to establish finance subsidiaries to issue securities for the parent institution

(Appendix C continues)

Item and Date	Key Provisions
Mutual-to-stock conversion (August 1984)	Imposed a 3-year restriction on the acquisition of the stock of recently converted institutions
Brokered deposits (February 1985)	Limited the amount of brokered deposits to 5 percent of deposits at FSLIC-insured institutions failing to meet their "regulatory network requirement"; permitted principal supervisory agents to make exceptions.
Direct investment (February 1985)	Limited the investment by FSLIC-insured institutions in direct investments (equity securities, real estate, service corporations, and operating subsidiaries) to the greater of 10 percent of assets or twice the institution's net worth, provided that the institution meets its regulatory and special-purpose net-worth requirements; limited the direct investments of institutions that meet their regulatory net-worth requirement, but not their special-purpose net-worth requirement, to twice the institution's net worth; restricted institutions that fail to meet their minimum net-worth requirement from making direct investments, except as approved by their principal supervisory agent
Special assessment (March 1985)	Ordered the assessment of an additional premium ($\frac{1}{8}$ of 1 percent annually) against FSLIC-insured institutions for the first time
Management consignment program (April 1985)	Introduced the Management Consignment Program whereby the bank board may take formal action to replace the boards of directors or the management of

Item and Date	*Key Provisions*
	insolvent institutions in the FSLIC's caseload without arranging a resolution
Financial options transactions (April 1985)	Permitted FSLIC-insured institutions to enter over-the-counter financial options transactions with primary dealers in government securities and those affiliated companies substantially engaged in similar activities, provided that the primary dealer guarantees the transactions entered into by its affiliates
Classification of assets (December 1985)	Permitted examiners of FSLIC-insured institutions to classify questionable loans and other assets for the purpose of requiring general and specific reserve allocations. Problem assets are to be classified as "substandard," "doubtful," or "loss" based on the degree of the risk of nonpayment. An institution's minimum net-worth requirement is to be increased 20 percent of the value of its "substandard" assets. Assets classified "doubtful" or "loss" require specific reserves of 50 percent and 100 percent of the value of the assets, respectively. The classification system applies to all assets except loans secured by one- to four-family, owner-occupied homes, consumer credit, and securities.
Classification of assets (January 1988)	Broadened the scope of assets to include all assets of FSLIC-insured institutions. Examiners are given the authority to identify problem assets and to classify them. Each insured institution is required to classify its own assets regularly

(Appendix C continues)

Item and Date	Key Provisions
	and to provide aggregate totals in its quarterly reports to the bank board. Asset evaluations that are consistent with the practice of the federal banking agencies may be used for supervisory purposes. Adequate valuation allowances consistent with generally accepted accounting principles shall be established for classified assets.
Southwest Plan (February 1988)	Introduced the Southwest Plan, a program to consolidate and "package" unhealthy institutions in the Southwest

SOURCE: Barth and Bradley (1989).

APPENDIX D:

HISTORY OF THE REGULATORY CAPITAL REQUIREMENT FOR SAVINGS AND LOANS IN THE 1980s

Date	Regulatory Change
January 1980	The FHLBB required institutions to hold two types of reserves, statutory and regulatory.[a] Each insured institution was required to establish a statutory reserve that it increased each year by a stated percentage and that at the end of twenty-six years would be equal to 5 percent of its insured accounts, defined as checking and savings accounts. In addition, each insured institution was required to meet a net worth requirement and to build up its net worth so that at the end of each year, net worth equaled the *greater* of two amounts: one was calculated on the basis of an institution's statutory reserve requirement, its scheduled items, and secured borrowings with an original stated maturity in excess of one year;[b] the other was calculated using the Asset Composition and Net Worth Index, which assigned minimum net worth percentage to categories of assets held by insured institutions.[c] Items that an institution could use to satisfy its net worth requirement included all reserve accounts (except specific or valuation reserves), retained earnings, capital stock, the principal amount of any subordinated debt securities (up to 20 percent of its net worth requirement), and any other nonwithdrawable accounts of an insured institution.
March 1980	The Depository Institutions Deregulation and Monetary Control Act of 1980 replaced the statutory reserve requirement of 5 percent of insured deposits with a range of 3 percent to

(Appendix D continues)

133

Date	Regulatory Change
	6 percent of insured deposits, the specific percentage to be established by the FHLBB. The act also provided that mutual capital certificates could be used as part of the statutory reserve of issuing mutual institutions.
July 1980	The FHLBB directed that the statutory reserve was to be used specifically for the absorption of losses, including bad debts. Subordinated debentures and specific loss reserves were excluded from the list of items that an institution could use to satisfy its net worth requirement. The FHLBB reduced to twenty years the period at the end of which all insured institutions were required to meet the statutory reserve requirement of 5 percent.
November 1980	The FHLBB reduced the statutory reserve requirement to 4 percent of insured deposits. It also eliminated the former net worth requirement calculations and replaced them with the sum of 4 percent of total liabilities plus an amount equal to 20 percent of the institution's scheduled items. A "qualifying balance deduction" was established that reduced an institution's net worth requirement by up to 10 percent. The amount of the deduction was proportionate to the amount of qualifying balances held by an institution.[d] The FHLBB provided a limited exemption from the net worth and statutory reserve requirements for institutions that sold mortgages carrying an interest rate equal to or less than 7.5 percent and provided that mutual capital certificates could constitute up to 20 percent of the statutory reserve and up to 20 percent of the net worth amount of the issuing insured mutual institutions.[e] The FHLBB clarified that only permanent stock

Date	Regulatory Change
	could be used to meet the statutory reserve and net worth requirements.[f]
September 1981	The FHLBB permitted troubled institutions to issue special securities, income capital certificates, that were to be purchased by the FSLIC (either with cash or interest-bearing FSLIC notes) and included in net worth by the issuing institution.
September 1981	The FHLBB permitted insured institutions to defer and amortize gains and losses on the sale or other disposition of mortgage loans, mortgage-related securities, and debt securities. Exemptions from the net worth and statutory reserve requirements were expanded to include institutions that incurred losses on the sale or other disposition of mortgage loans, mortgage-related securities, and debt securities.
January 1982	The FHLBB reduced the statutory reserve requirement to 3 percent of insured accounts, and the net worth requirement to 3 percent of liabilities.
July 1982	The FHLBB approved accounting changes that allowed the goodwill of an acquired institution to be expensed over a long period (forty years) while the income realized from the difference between the book and the market value of assets could be accumulated over a short period (five to ten years).
July 1982	The FHLBB excluded contra-asset accounts from the total liabilities base of the net worth calculation.[g]

(Appendix D continues)

Date	Regulatory Change
August 1982	The FHLBB permitted insured institutions to include the full amount of any subordinated debt securities, redeemable mutual capital certificates, and nonpermanent preferred stock having a remaining term to maturity or term to redemption exceeding one year in fulfilling its statutory reserve and net worth requirements.
November 1982	The FHLBB permitted insured institutions to include "appraised equity capital" as part of their reserves.[h]
December 1982	The Garn-St Germain Depository Institutions Act of 1982 added net worth certificates to the list of items included under the term "reserves" and to the list of items to which losses could be charged under the statutory reserve requirement. The act also deleted the 3 to 6 percent range within which the FHLBB was required to set the statutory reserve percentage and the twenty- to thirty-year phase-in period, substituting instead the requirement that an insured institution "will provide adequate reserves in a form satisfactory to the Corporation, to be established in regulation made by the Corporation."
February 1983	The FHLBB ruled that once the FSLIC purchases net worth certificates from a qualified institution, the FSLIC is committed under certain circumstances to purchase additional net worth certificates from that institution.
November 1983	The FHLBB required newly chartered institutions to hold statutory reserves at 7 percent of insured accounts and net worth at 7 percent of liabilities for the first full fiscal year, with

Date	Regulatory Change
	the requirements to decrease gradually to 3 percent of deposits and 3 percent of liabilities.
September 1984	The FHLBB increased the maximum amount of net worth certificates that the FSLIC could purchase from a qualified institution and clarified certain policy objectives of the program.
January 1985	The FHLBB replaced the separate statutory reserve and regulatory net worth requirements with a single revised net worth that used a combination of four "factors" to calculate the minimum net worth requirement. This requirement was equal to the sum of the base factor, the amortization factor, the growth factor, and a contingency factor.[i] The institution then reduced the sum of these four factors by the amount of its qualifying balance deduction, but could not reduce it by more than 10 percent of its otherwise applicable requirement.[j] The new calculation required each institution to calculate its minimum net worth requirement at the end of each calendar quarter.
April 1985	The FHLBB provided a schedule to amortize subordinated debt issued *after* December 5, 1985, and included as net worth.[k] Subordinated debt issued prior to December 5, 1984, could be fully included as regulatory net worth until the remaining time to maturity was less than one year. Subordinated debt securities sold to other FSLIC-insured institutions or their corporate affiliates were excluded from regulatory net worth.
October 1985	The FHLBB permitted, under specified circumstances, nonpermanent preferred stock to be included as regulatory net worth.[l]

(Appendix D continues)

137

APPENDIX D (continued)

Date	Regulatory Change
August 1986	The FHLBB replaced the four "factors" used to calculate the minimum net worth requirement with a capital requirement that consisted of a liability component plus a contingency component, from which a maturity matching credit was subtracted. The liability component required an insured institution to hold capital equal to 6 percent of liabilities. Growth was to be capitalized immediately at 6 percent, but institutions were permitted a number of years to achieve 6 percent capital on their existing liabilities. The initial minimum capital requirement was set equal to that under the former net worth regulation. This minimum amount was to be increased annually by a fraction of the average profitability in the industry during the previous year until it equaled 6 percent. The contingency component allowed an institution to reduce its capital requirement by having one-year and three-year hedged maturity gaps in selected ranges.[m]
August 1987	The Competitive Equality Banking Act of 1987 enabled the FHLBB to alter minimum capital requirements with respect to an individual institution as is necessary or appropriate in light of the particular circumstances of that institution. In addition, the FHLBB was given authorization to issue a directive requiring an institution to increase its capital.
December 1987	The FHLBB set forth discretionary standards for determination of appropriate individual capital requirements. The FHLBB set forth the conditions and circumstances under which a capital directive will be issued to an insured institution.

138

APPENDIX D (continued)

Date	Regulatory Change
April 1988	The FHLBB altered the calculation of the required increase in capital, basing the increase on median profitability rather than average industry profitability.

a. The calculations of minimum reserve requirements permitted the use of five-year averaging and twenty-year phase-in techniques.

b. This amount equaled the sum of the institution's statutory requirement, plus an amount equal to 20 percent of the institution's scheduled items, plus an amount equal to 5 percent of all outstanding secured borrowings with an original stated maturity in excess of one year.

c. The minimum net worth percentages ranged from 15 percent for unsecured consumer loans to 2 percent for insured or guaranteed loans. Before the minimum net worth percentage was applied to an asset, the amount of the asset could be reduced by any applicable allowances or reserves for depreciation, valuation allowance or reserve, specific reserve or loss reserve, and any applicable loans in process. Any deferred income or accrued interest associated with any asset was included with the asset.

d. The deduction included up to 50 percent of adjustable-rate mortgages, interest-bearing liquid assets, and fixed-rate liabilities with a term to maturity of more than five years.

e. The aggregate amount of all outstanding and proposed redeemable mutual capital certificates could not exceed 20 percent of the institution's net worth.

f. Redeemable stock was included in reserves in certain FSLIC-approved mergers, consolidations or reorganizations.

g. A contra-asset is a deduction from a specific asset account, carried as a separate account for bookkeeping purposes. Specifically, the bank board ruled that assets entitled "loans in process," "specific reserves," and all "deferred credits" (except deferred taxes) may be considered contra-asset accounts rather than liabilities.

h. Appraised equity equals the difference between the book value and the appraised fair market value of selected eligible office land, buildings, and improvements, including leasehold improvements, owned by an insured institution or any of its subsidiaries.

(Appendix D continues)

139

i. The base factor was the institution's minimum net worth requirement as of the preceding December 31 less the contingency factor and before the reduction for qualifying balances. The amortization factor was the difference between the use of the five-year averaging and twenty-year phase-in techniques in calculating the base factor for 1985 and not using these techniques as of December 31, 1984, amortized quarterly over five years. The contingency factor was an amount equal to the sum of: 2 percent of the loans sold with recourse against the institution; 20 percent of the institution's scheduled items; and 10 percent of the institution's direct investments (excluding grandfathered investments) that exceeded the greater of 10 percent of assets or twice regulatory net worth. The growth factor varied from 2.34 percent to 5 percent depending on an institution's size and growth rate, defined on the basis of the institution's increase in total liabilities from the beginning of a calendar year to the end of the quarter for which the computations are made.

j. Rules for calculating additional net worth applied for institutions that merged or purchased substantially all the liabilities of another institution.

k. The amount includable as net worth had to be amortized pursuant to a schedule that permitted 100 percent to be included when the years to maturity are greater than or equal to seven and decreased by approximately $\frac{1}{7}$ each year thereafter.

l. Redeemable preferred stock could be included as regulatory net worth, but only if such inclusion had been approved by the FSLIC. In addition, the amount of redeemable preferred stock that could be included was subjected to an amortization schedule that reduced the amount of the stock that could be included if it was owned by a service corporation or subsidiary controlled by the issuing insured institution.

m. The contingency component classified "risky" assets as fixed-reserve elements or variable-reserve elements. With respect to certain fixed reserve elements, there was a 2 percent requirement on recourse liabilities, a 2 percent requirement on standby letters of credit, and a 20 percent requirement on scheduled items. The requirement on a variable-reserve element depended on an institution's actual capital level and its concentration in a specific asset category. The variable-reserve elements included land loans, direct investments, and nonresidential construction loans. The requirement on direct investments ranged from 0 to 10 percent, and from 0 to 4 percent on land loans and nonresidential construction loans. The maturity-matching credit allowed an institution

140

to reduce its capital requirement by up to 2 percent of liabilities for one-year and three-year hedged maturity gaps of less than 15 percent absolute value. Gaps between 15 and 25 percent received credit on a declining scale and gaps above 25 percent received no credit. An institution could not use the maturity-matching credit to bring its overall requirement below 3 percent for the first three years that the regulation was in effect and not below 4 percent thereafter.

SOURCE: Barth and Bradley (1989).

APPENDIX E:

CHRONOLOGY OF THE FINANCIAL INSTITUTIONS REFORM, RECOVERY, AND ENFORCEMENT ACT, FEBRUARY–AUGUST 1989

February 6   President Bush announced his plan to resolve the crisis in the savings and loan industry and to place federal deposit insurance on a sound basis. As proposed, the plan would create and fund a new corporation to pay the cost of closing all insolvent institutions, reorganize the regulatory structure of the industry, and restrict the activities while simultaneously increasing the capital requirements of insured institutions.

April 19   The Senate approved its version of the savings and loan rescue and reform bill (S. 774) that was very close in spirit to the administration's plan.

June 15   The House adopted its version of the bill (H.R. 1278), including on-budget financing, tougher capital standards, and affordable housing programs.

July 27   Congressional conferees completed their work on the bill and agreed to include the $50 billion funding program in the federal budget while exempting the resulting three-year increase in the federal deficit from the Balanced Budget and Emergency Deficit Control Act of 1985, amended in 1987 (commonly known as Gramm-Rudman-Hollings).

August 3   President Bush wrote letters to House minority leader Robert Michel of Illinois and Senate minority leader Robert Dole of Kansas, threatening to veto the bill if the funding program was placed on budget.

August 3   Despite the veto threat, the House approved the conference report.

August 3   The Senate turned down the conference report when it failed by a vote of 54 to 46 to achieve the three-fifths majority needed to grant the budget treatment an exemption from Gramm-Rudman-Hollings. The bill was immediately returned to conference to resolve the only remaining point of con-

	tention—the budgeting treatment of the financing plan.
August 4	The Senate accepted the revised conference report that placed $20 billion on budget in 1989 and $30 billion off budget in fiscal years 1990 and 1991.
August 5	The House accepted the revised conference report with the House leadership placing many of the proxy votes for members that had begun the summer recess.
August 9	President Bush signed FIRREA into law.

SOURCE: Office of Thrift Supervision.

143

APPENDIX F:

HISTORY OF FEDERAL DEPOSIT INSURANCE PREMIUMS AND COVERAGE, 1934–1989

	Savings and Loans		Commercial Banks
June 27, 1934 National Housing Act	An annual premium set at $\frac{1}{4}$ of 1% of total insured deposits. An annual special assessment of $\frac{1}{4}$ of 1% may also be levied to cover insolvency losses. Insurance coverage set at $5,000 per depositor per insured institution.	June 16, 1933 Banking Act of 1933	Under a temporary insurance plan, the premium is set at $\frac{1}{2}$ of 1% of total insured deposits. Half the total assessment to be paid in full upon admission to the fund, with the remainder subject to call. A special assessment is not to exceed the amount already paid in for that year, for a possible maximum special assessment of $\frac{1}{2}$ of 1% of total insured deposits. Insurance coverage set at $2,500 per depositor per insured institution.
May 28, 1935 An Act to Provide Additional Home-Mortgage Relief	The annual premium reduced to $\frac{1}{8}$ of 1%. The maximum special assessment also reduced to $\frac{1}{8}$ of 1%.		
June 27, 1950 Amendment to the National Housing Act	The annual premium reduced to $\frac{1}{12}$ of 1%, but the special assessment remains at $\frac{1}{8}$ of 1%. A line of credit with the Treasury Department is	August 23, 1935 Banking Act of 1935	Under the permanent insurance plan, the premium is assessed on *total* domestic

144

September 8, 1961 Amendment to National Housing Act	established, with the maximum amount borrowable in an emergency set at $750 million. Insurance coverage is set at $10,000 per individual depositor. Establishment of a secondary reserve, a prepayment reserve with a 2% annual assessment on anticipated net increases in total deposits.
October 16, 1966 Financial Institutions Supervisory Act	Insurance coverage set at $15,000 per individual depositor.
December 23, 1969 Credit Control Act	Insurance coverage set at $20,000 per individual depositor.
August 5, 1947 Banking Act of 1935	deposits and reduced to $\frac{1}{12}$ of 1% per annum. Maximum emergency borrowings from the Treasury Department are $975 million, and the special assessment power is eliminated. The line of credit at the Treasury Department increased to $3 billion.
September 21, 1950 Federal Deposit Insurance Act	Premium rebates equal to 60% of net assessment income as established. Insurance coverage set at $10,000 per individual depositor.
July 14, 1960 Amendment to	Rebates increased to 66.66% of net assessment income.

(Appendix F continues)

145

APPENDIX F (continued)

Savings and Loans		Commercial Banks	
August 16, 1973 Amendment to National Housing Act	Eliminates payments into the prepayment reserve or the secondary reserve.	Federal Deposit Insurance Act	
October 28, 1974 Act of October 28, 1974	Insurance coverage set at $40,000 per individual depositor.	October 16, 1966 Financial Institutions Supervisory Act	Insurance coverage set at $15,000 per individual depositor.
March 31, 1980 Depository Institutions Deregulation and Monetary Control Act	Insurance coverage set at $100,000 per individual depositor.	December 23, 1969 Credit Control Act	Insurance coverage set at $20,000 per individual depositor.
March 31, 1985	The special assessment of $\frac{1}{8}$ of 1% annually levied for first time.	October 28, 1974 Act of October 28, 1974	Insurance coverage set at $40,000 per individual depositor. Insurance coverage for time and savings accounts held by state and political subdivisions set at $100,000.

August 9, 1989 Financial Institutions Reform, Recovery, and Enforcement Act	The SAIF replaces the FSLIC. Annual premium set at $5/24$ of 1% in 1990 ($1/12$ of 1% plus the special assessment of $1/8$ of 1%), $23/100$ of 1% in 1991–93, $18/100$ of 1% in 1994–97, and $15/100$ of 1% in 1998 and after.
November 10, 1978 Financial Institutions Regulatory and Interest Rate Act of 1978	Insurance coverage for IRA and Keough accounts set at $100,000.
March 31, 1980 Depository Institutions Deregulation and Monetary Control Act	Rebates decreased to 60% of net assessment income. Insurance coverage set at $100,000 per individual depositor.
August 9, 1989 Financial Institutions Reform, Recovery, and Enforcement Act	The BIF replaces the Permanent Insurance Fund. Annual premium set at $12/100$ of 1% in 1990 and $15/100$ of 1% after 1990. In 1998, both BIF and SAIF to have same premium.

SOURCE: Adapted from Barth, Bradley, and Feid (1989).

Bibliography

American Bankers Association. *Federal Deposit Insurance: A Program for Reform.* Washington, D.C., March 1990.

Anderson, John. "The Next S&L Failures." *Washington Post,* July 3, 1985.

Association of Bank Holding Companies. "Policy Recommendations on Federal Deposit Insurance." U.S. Department of Treasury, March 9, 1990.

Avery, Robert B., Gerald A. Hanweck, and Myron L. Kwast. "An Analysis of Risk-based Deposit Insurance for Commercial Banks." *Bank Structure and Competition.* Federal Reserve Bank of Chicago: 1985.

Baer, Herbert L. "Foreign Competition in U.S. Banking Markets." *Economic Perspectives.* Federal Reserve Bank of Chicago, May/June 1990.

———. "Private Prices, Public Insurance: The Pricing of Federal Deposit Insurance." *Economic Perspectives.* Federal Reserve Bank of Chicago, September/October 1986.

Barth, James R. "Post FIRREA: The Need to Reform the Federal Deposit Insurance System." Paper presented at the Twenty-sixth Annual Conference on Bank Structure and Competition, Federal Reserve Bank of Chicago, May 9–11, 1990.

———. Statement before the House Committee on Banking, Finance, and Urban Affairs. 101st Congress, 2d session. April 11, 1990.

———. Statement before the Senate Committee on Banking, Housing, and Urban Affairs. 101st Congress, 2d session. May 22, 1990.

Barth, James R., and Philip F. Bartholomew. "The Thrift-Industry Crisis: Revealed Weaknesses in the Federal Deposit Insurance System." Paper presented at conference, Reform of Deposit Insurance and the Regulation of Depository Institutions in the 1990s: Setting the Agenda. Center for Economic Policy Research, Stanford University, May 18–19, 1990.

149

Barth, James R., Philip F. Bartholomew, and Michael G. Bradley. "Determinants of Thrift Institution Resolution Costs." *Journal of Finance*, 45(July 1990):731–54.

———. "Reforming Federal Deposit Insurance: What Can Be Learned from Private Insurance Practices?" *Consumer Finance Law Quarterly Report*, forthcoming.

Barth, James R., Philip F. Bartholomew, and Peter J. Elmer. "The Cost of Liquidating versus Selling Failed Thrift Institutions." Research Paper No. 89-02, Office of the Chief Economist, Office of Thrift Supervision, November 1989.

Barth, James R., Philip F. Bartholomew, and Carol J. Labich. "Moral Hazard and the Thrift Crisis: An Analysis of 1988 Resolutions." *Bank Structure and Competition*. Federal Reserve Bank of Chicago: 1989.

Barth, James R., George J. Benston, and Philip R. Wiest. "The Financial Institutions Reform, Recovery, and Enforcement Act of 1989: Description, Effects, and Implications." *Issues in Bank Regulation* 13(Winter 1990):3–11.

Barth, James R., and Michael G. Bradley. "Thrift Deregulation and Federal Deposit Insurance." *Journal of Financial Services Research* 2(September 1989):231–59.

Barth, James R., Michael G. Bradley, and John J. Feid. "How Deposit Insurance Went Awry." *Federal Home Loan Bank Board Journal* 19(February 1989):15–19.

Barth, James R., and R. Dan Brumbaugh, Jr. "The Continuing Bungling of the Savings and Loan Crisis: The Rough Road from FIRREA to the Reform of Deposit Insurance." *Stanford Law and Policy Review* 2(Spring 1990):58–67.

Barth, James R., R. Dan Brumbaugh, Jr., and Daniel Sauerhaft. "Failure Costs of Government-Regulated Financial Firms: The Case of Thrift Institutions." Research Working Paper No. 132, Office of Policy and Economic Research, Federal Home Loan Bank Board, October 1986.

Barth, James R., R. Dan Brumbaugh, Jr., Daniel Sauerhaft, and George H. K. Wang. "Insolvency and Risk-taking in the Thrift Industry: Implications for the Future." *Contemporary Policy Issues* 3(Fall 1985): 1–32.

———. "Thrift-Institution Failures: Causes and Policy Issues." In *Bank Structure and Competition*. Federal Reserve Bank of Chicago: 1985.

———. "Thrift-Institution Failures: Estimating the Regulator's Closure Rule." In *Research in Financial Services*, vol. 1. Edited by George G. Kaufman. Greenwich, Conn.: JAI Press, 1989.

Barth, James R., John J. Feid, Gabriel Riedel, and H. Hampton Tunis.

BIBLIOGRAPHY

"Alternative Federal Deposit Insurance Regimes." *Problems of the Federal Savings and Loan Insurance Corporation.* Hearings before the Senate Committee on Banking, Housing, and Urban Affairs. 101st Congress, 1st session. Part IV, 1989.

Barth, James R., and James L. Freund. "The Evolving Financial Services Sector, 1970–1988." Office of Thrift Supervision, September 1989. Mimeo.

Barth, James R., and Robert E. Keleher. "'Financial Crises' and the Role of the Lender of Last Resort." *Economic Review,* Federal Reserve Bank of Atlanta, 69(January 1984):58–67.

Barth, James R., and Martin A. Regalia. "The Evolving Role of Regulation in the Savings and Loan Industry." In *The Financial Services Revolution: Policy Directions for the Future.* Edited by Catherine England and Thomas Huertas. Norwell, Mass.: Kluwer Academic Publishers, 1988.

Barth, James R., Daniel E. Page, and R. Dan Brumbaugh, Jr. "What Do Stock Prices Tell Us about the Financial Conditions of Federally Insured Thrift Institutions?" September 1990. Mimeo.

Bartholomew, Philip F. "Foreign Deposit Insurance Systems." *Special Report.* Federal Home Loan Bank Board, March 1989.

———. "How Some Nations Regulate Depository Institutions." *Office of Thrift Supervision Journal* 19(October 1989):20–23.

———. "Recent Developments for Canadian 'Near Banks.'" *Housing Finance International* 4(August 1989):28–31.

Bartholomew, Philip F., and Vicki A. Vanderhoff. "Foreign Deposit Insurance Systems: A Comparison." *Consumer Finance Law Quarterly Report,* forthcoming.

Beaver, William H., Srikant Datar, and Mark A. Wolfson. "The Role of Market Value Accounting in the Regulation of Insured Depository Institutions." 1990. Mimeo.

Benston, George J. *An Analysis of the Causes of Savings and Loan Association Failures.* Monograph Series in Finance and Economics No. 1985-4/5. Salomon Brothers Center for the Study of Financial Institutions, Graduate School of Business Administration, New York University, 1985.

———. "Direct Investments and FSLIC Losses." In *Research in Financial Services,* vol. I. Edited by George G. Kaufman. Greenwich, Conn.: JAI Press, 1989.

———. "Market Value Accounting: Benefits, Costs, and Incentives." *Banking System Risk: Charting a New Course.* Federal Reserve Bank of Chicago: 1989.

———. "The Federal 'Safety Net' and the Repeal of the Glass-Steagall's

151

Separation of Commercial and Investment Banking." *Journal of Financial Services Research* 2(September 1989):287–305.

———. "U.S. Banking in an Increasingly Integrated and Competitive World Economy." Paper presented at conference, International Competitiveness in the Financial Services. American Enterprise Institute, May 31–June 1, 1990.

Benston, George J., et al. *Blueprint for Restructuring America's Financial Institutions*. Washington, D.C.: Brookings Institution, 1989.

———. *Perspectives on Safe and Sound Banking: Past, Present, and Future*. Cambridge, Mass.: MIT Press, 1986.

Benston, George J., Mike Carhill, and Brian Olasov. "Market-Value vs. Historical Cost Accounting: Evidence from Southeastern Thrifts." Paper presented at conference, Reform of Deposit Insurance and the Regulation of Depository Institutions in the 1990s: Setting the Agenda. Center for Economic Policy Research, Stanford University, May 18–19, 1990.

Benston, George J., and George G. Kaufman. "Regulating Bank Safety and Performance." *Restructuring Banking and Financial Services in America*. Edited by William S. Haraf and Rose Marie Kushmeider. Washington, D.C.: American Enterprise Institute, 1988.

———. "Risk and Solvency Regulation of Depository Institutions." Salomon Brothers Center for the Study of Financial Institutions, Graduate School of Business Administration, New York University, 1988.

Benston, George J., and Michael Koehn. "Capital Dissipation, Deregulation, and the Insolvency of Thrifts." 1988. Mimeo.

Berger, Allen N., Kathleen A. Kuester, and James M. O'Brien. "Some Red Flags concerning Market Value Accounting." *Banking System Risk: Charting a New Course*. Federal Reserve Bank of Chicago: 1989.

Bernheim, B. Douglas. "The Crisis in Deposit Insurance: Issues and Options." *Capital Issues in Banking*. Washington, D.C.: Association of Reserve City Bankers. 1988.

Bisenius, Donald J., R. Dan Brumbaugh, Jr., and Ronald C. Rogers. "Insolvent Thrift Institutions, Agency Issues, and the Management Consignment Program." Research Paper No. 141, Office of Policy and Economic Research, Federal Home Loan Bank Board, April 1988.

Blacconiere, Walter G. "Accounting Regulations in the Savings and Loan Industry: Evidence of Market Reactions and Implications of Contracting." Center for Accounting Research, University of Southern California, 1989.

Black, William K. "Ending Our Forbearers' Forbearances: FIRREA and Supervisory Goodwill." *Stanford Law and Policy Review* 2(Spring 1990):102–16.

BIBLIOGRAPHY

————. Statement concerning Lincoln Savings and Loan Association before the House Committee on Banking, Finance, and Urban Affairs. 101st Congress, 1st session.

————. Statement on the Effectiveness of Law Enforcement against Financial Crime before the House Committee on Banking, Finance, and Urban Affairs. 101st Congress, 2d session. April 11,1990.

Bodfish, Morton. *History of Building and Loans in the United States.* Chicago: U.S. Building and Loan League, 1931.

Bodfish, Morton, and A. D. Theobald. *Savings and Loan Principles.* New York: Prentice-Hall, Inc., 1940.

Bordo, Michael D. "The Lender of Last Resort: Some Historical Perspectives." Working Paper No. 3011, National Bureau of Economic Research, July 1989.

Bosworth, Barry P., Andrew S. Carron, and Elizabeth H. Rhyne. *The Economics of Federal Credit Programs.* Washington, D.C.: Brookings Institution, 1987.

Bovenzie, John F., and Arthur J. Murton. "Resolution Costs and Bank Failures." *FDIC Banking Review* 6(Fall 1988):1–13.

Bower, Linda E., A. Frank Thompson, and Venkat Srinivasan. "The Ohio Banking Crisis: A Lesson in Consumer Finance." *Journal of Consumer Affairs* 20(Winter 1986):290–99.

Boyd, John H., and Arthur J. Rolnik. "A Case for Reforming Federal Deposit Insurance." *Annual Report.* Federal Reserve Bank of Minneapolis: 1988.

Breeden, Richard C. Statement before the Senate Committee on Banking, Housing, and Urban Affairs. 101st Congress, 2d session. July 19, 1990.

Bremer, C. D. *American Bank Failures.* New York: AMS Press, Inc., 1935.

Brewer III, Elijah. "Full-blown Crisis, Half-Measure Cure." *Economic Perspectives*, Federal Reserve Bank of Chicago, November/December 1989.

————. "The Impact of Deposit Insurance on S&L Shareholders' Risk/Return Trade-Offs." Working Paper on Issues in Financial Regulation, No. 1989/24, Federal Reserve Bank of Chicago, May 1990.

Brewer III, Elijah, et al. "The Depository Institutions Deregulation and Monetary Control Act of 1980." *Economic Perspectives*, Federal Reserve Bank of Chicago, September/October 1980.

Brickley, James A., and Christopher M. James. "Access to Deposit Insurance, Insolvency Rules and the Stock Returns of Financial Institutions." *Journal of Financial Economics* 16(1986):345–71.

153

Brookings Institution. *Restructuring America's Financial Institutions.* Report of a Task Force, 1989.

Brumbaugh, R. Dan, Jr. Statement before the House Committee on Banking, Finance, and Urban Affairs. 101st Congress, 2d session. January 25, 1990.

––––––. *Thrifts under Siege.* Cambridge, Mass.: Ballinger Publishing Co., 1988.

Brumbaugh, R. Dan, Jr., and Andrew S. Carron. "Thrift Industry Crisis: Causes and Solutions." *Brookings Papers on Economic Activity,* 1987.

Brumbaugh, R. Dan, Jr., Andrew S. Carron, and Robert E. Litan. "Cleaning Up the Depository Institutions Mess." *Brookings Papers on Economic Activity,* 1989.

Brumbaugh, R. Dan, Jr., and Eric I. Hemel. "Federal Deposit Insurance as a Call Option: Implications for Depository Institutions." Research Working Paper No. 116, Office of Policy and Economic Research, Federal Home Loan Bank Board, October 1984.

Brumbaugh, R. Dan, Jr., and Robert E. Litan. "A Critique of the Financial Institutions Reform, Recovery, and Enforcement Act of 1989 and the Financial Strength of the Commercial Banks." Paper presented at conference, Reform of Deposit Insurance and the Regulation of Depository Institutions in the 1990s: Setting the Agenda. Center for Economic Policy Research, Stanford University, May 18–19, 1990.

––––––. "Seeds of Crisis are Present in the Banking Industry." *American Banker,* October 11, 1989.

––––––. "The Banks Are Worse Off Than You Think." *Challenge* 33(January/February 1990):4–12.

––––––. "The S&L Crisis: How to Get Out and Stay Out." *Brookings Review* (Spring 1989):3–15.

Bryan, Lowell L. *Breaking Up the Bank.* Homewood, Ill.: Dow Jones-Irwin, 1988.

Burnham, James B. "A Financial System for the Year 2000: The Case for Narrow Banking." Center for the Study of American Business, Washington University, February 1990.

Buser, Stephen A., Andrew W. Chen, and Edward J. Kane. "Federal Deposit Insurance, Regulatory Policy, and Optimal Bank Capital." *Journal of Finance* 36(March 1981):51–60.

Caliguire, Daria B., and James B. Thompson. "FDIC Policies for Dealing with Failed and Troubled Institutions." *Economic Commentary,* Federal Reserve Bank of Cleveland, October 1, 1987.

154

Calomiris, Charles W. "Deposit Insurance: Lessons from the Record." *Economic Perspectives*, Federal Reserve Bank of Chicago, May/June 1989.

―――. "Do 'Vulnerable' Economies Need Deposit Insurance?: Lessons from the U.S. Agricultural Boom and Bust of 1920s." Working Paper Series, Federal Reserve Bank of Chicago, 1989.

―――. "Getting the Incentives Right in the Current Deposit Insurance System: Successes from the Pre-FDIC Era." Paper presented at conference, Reform of Deposit Insurance and the Regulation of Depository Institutions in the 1990s: Setting the Agenda. Center for Economic Policy Research, Stanford University, May 18–19, 1990.

―――. "Is Deposit Insurance Necessary?: A Historical Perspective." *Journal of Economic History*, forthcoming.

―――. "Success and Failure in Pre-Depression Bank Liability Insurance." *Banking System Risk: Charting a New Course*. Federal Reserve Bank of Chicago: 1989.

Cargill, Thomas F. "Financial Reform in the United States and Japan: Comparative View." *Financial Policy and Reform in Pacific Basin Countries*. Edited by Hang-Sheng Cheng. Lexington, Mass.: Lexington Books, 1986.

Cargill, Thomas F., and Shoichi Royama. "The Evolution of Japanese Banking: Isolation to Globalization." *Bank Structure and Competition*. Federal Reserve Bank of Chicago: 1990.

―――. *The Transition of Finance in Japan and the United States: A Comparative Perspective*. Stanford, Calif.: Hoover Institution Press, 1988.

Carns, Frederick S. "Should the $100,000 Deposit Insurance Limit Be Changed?" *FDIC Banking Review* (Spring/Summer 1989).

Carron, Andrew S. "Overseas Financial Sector Deregulation: Lessons from Australia and New Zealand." *Bank Structure and Competition*. Federal Reserve Bank of Chicago: May 1985.

―――. *The Plight of the Thrift Institutions*. Washington, D.C.: Brookings Institution, 1982.

―――. "The Political Economy of Financial Regulation." *The Political Economy of Deregulation*. Edited by Roger G. Noll and Bruce Owen. Washington, D.C.: American Enterprise Institute, 1983.

Carron, Andrew S., and R. Dan Brumbaugh, Jr. "The Future of Thrifts in the Mortgage Market." *Banking System Risk: Charting a New Course*. Federal Reserve Bank of Chicago, 1989.

―――. "The Viability of the Thrift Industry." *Housing Policy Debate*, Federal National Mortgage Association, Summer 1990.

Casey, Diane M. "Assessing Foreign Deposits: The Controversy." *Independent Banker*, August 1989.

Chan, Yuk-Shee, Stuart I. Greenbaum, and Anjan V. Thakor. "Is Fairly Priced Deposit Insurance Possible?" Working Paper No. 152, Banking Reserve Center, Kellogg Graduate School of Management, Northwestern University, October 1988.

Chari, V. V. "Banking without Deposit Insurance or Bank Panics: Lessons from a Model of the U.S. National Banking System." *Quarterly Review*, Federal Reserve Bank of Minneapolis, Summer 1989.

―――. "Time Consistency and Optimal Policy Design." *Quarterly Review*, Federal Reserve Bank of Minneapolis, Fall 1988.

Chirinko, Robert S., and Gene D. Guill. "Aggregate Stocks, Loan Losses, and Portfolio Concentrations: Lessons from Assessing Depository Institution Risk." Paper prepared for conference, Reform of Deposit Insurance and the Regulation of Depository Institutions in the 1990s: Setting the Agenda. Center for Economic Policy Research, Stanford University, Washington, D.C., May 18–19, 1990.

Congressional Budget Office. *Reducing the Deficit: Spending and Revenue Options.* A Report to the Senate and House Committees on the Budget, Part II, February 1990.

―――. *Reforming Federal Deposit Insurance*, A Report to the House Committee on Banking. Finance, and Urban Affairs, September 1990.

Cook, Douglas O., and Lewis J. Spellman. "Federal Financial Guarantees and the Occasional Market Pricing of Default Risk." 1989. Mimeo.

―――. "Market Cynicism of Government Guarantees: The Waning Days of the FSLIC." January 1990. Mimeo.

―――. "Reducing Default Premia on Insured Deposits: The Policy Alternatives." *The Future of the Thrift Industry*. Federal Home Loan Bank of San Francisco: 1988.

Cornett, Marcia M., and Hassan Tehranian. "An Examination of the Impact of the Garn-St Germain Depository Institutions Act of 1982 on Commercial Banks and Savings and Loans." *Journal of Finance* 45(March 1990):95–111.

Corrigan, E. Gerald. Statement before the Senate Committee on Banking, Housing, and Urban Affairs. 101st Congress, 2d session. May 3, 1990.

Craine, Roger, and Richard W. Nelson. "Can Depository Institutions Be Regulated As If They Were Margin Accounts?" April 1990. Mimeo.

BIBLIOGRAPHY

Crowley, Leo T. *Statement on the Banking Act of 1935.* Presented to the House Committee on Banking and Currency. 74th Congress, 1st session.

Crutsinger, Martin. "Nearly One in Six Savings and Loans Considered Insolvent." Associated Press, July 26, 1985.

Diamond, Douglas W., and Philip H. Dybvig. "Bank Runs, Deposit Insurance, and Liquidity." *Journal of Political Economy* 91(June 1983).

Dotsey, Michael, and Anatoli Kuprianov." Reforming Deposit Insurance: Lessons from the Savings and Loan Crisis." *Economic Review,* Federal Reserve Bank of Richmond, March/April 1990.

Edwards, Linda N., and Franklin R. Edwards. "Measuring the Effectiveness of Regulation: The Case of Bank Entry Regulation." *Journal of Law & Economics* 17(October 1974):445–60.

Eichler, Ned. *The Thrift Debacle.* Berkeley, Calif.: University of California Press, 1989.

Eisenbeis, Robert A. "Bank Holding Companies and Public Policy." *Financial Services: The Changing Institutions and Government Policy.* Edited by George J. Benston. Englewood Cliffs, N.J.: Prentice Hall, 1983.

———. "Restructuring Banking." *Challenge* 33(January/February 1990):18–21.

Ely, Bert. "Making Deposit Insurance Safe through 100% Cross-Guarantees." National Chamber Foundation, United States Chamber of Commerce, 1989.

———. "Crime Accounts for Only 3% of the Cost of the S&L Mess." July 19, 1990. Mimeo.

———. "Yes—Private Sector Deposit Insurance Is a Viable Alternative to Federal Deposit Insurance!" *Bank Structure and Competition.* Federal Reserve Bank of Chicago: 1985.

Emerson, Guy. "Guaranty of Deposits under the Banking Act of 1933." *Quarterly Journal of Economics* 48(1934):299–44.

Engelke, George L. "Mark-to-Market Accounting: What *Is* Real Market Value?" *Financial Managers' Statement,* January/February 1990.

England, Catherine. "A Market Approach to the Savings and Loan Crisis." *An American Vision: Policies for the '90's.* Edited by Edward H. Crane and David Boaz. Washington, D.C.: Cato Institute, 1989.

———. "Federal Deposit Insurance Reform: The Road Not Taken." February 1990. Mimeo.

———. "Private Deposit Insurance: Stabilizing the Banking System." Policy Analysis, No. 54, Washington, D.C.: Cato Institute, 1985.

157

England, Catherine, and Thomas Huertas, eds. *The Financial Services Revolution*. Norwell, Mass.: Kluwer Academic Publishers, 1987.

Fabritius, M. Manfred, and William Borges. *Saving the Savings and Loan: The U.S. Thrift Industry and the Texas Experience, 1950–1988*. New York: Praeger, 1989.

Federal Deposit Insurance Corporation (FDIC). *Annual Report*, 1934.

———. *Deposit Insurance for the Nineties: Meeting the Challenge*. FDIC, January 4, 1989.

———. *Insurance in a Changing Environment*, FDIC, April 1983.

———. *The First Fifty Years: A History of the FDIC 1933–1983*. Washington, D.C., FDIC: 1985.

Federal Home Loan Bank Board (FHLBB). *Agenda for Reform, A Report on Deposit Insurance to the Congress*. Washington, D.C.: FHLBB, March 1983.

———. *Annual Reports*, 1982–1985.

———. "Report of the Expanded Task Force on Current Value Accounting." April 12, 1983. Mimeo.

Federal Reserve Bank of Chicago. *Annual Report*, 1989.

———. *The Financial Services Industry in the Year 2000*, May 1988.

Federal Reserve Bank of Minneapolis. *Annual Report*, 1990.

Fisher, Irving. Statement before the House Committee on Banking and Currency. 74th Congress, 1st session. 1935.

Flannery, Mark J. "Deposit Insurance Creates a Need for Bank Regulation." *Business Review*, Federal Reserve Bank of Philadelphia, January/February 1982.

———. "Pricing Deposit Insurance When the Insurer Measures Risk with Error." *Banking System Risk: Charting a New Course*. Federal Reserve Bank of Chicago: 1989.

Flannery, Mark J., and Christopher M. James. "The Effect of Interest Rate Changes of the Common Stock Returns of Financial Institutions." *Journal of Finance* 39(1984):1143–53.

———. "The Incidence of Deposit Insurance Subsidies and the Moral Hazard Problem in Banking." Annual Meeting of the American Economic Association. Atlanta, Georgia, December 1989.

Flannery, Mark J., and Aris A. Protopapadakis. "Risk-Sensitive Deposit Insurance Premia: Some Practical Issues." *Business Review*, Federal Reserve Bank of Philadelphia, September/October 1984, pp. 3–10.

Friedman, Milton, and Anna J. Schwartz. *A Monetary History of the United States, 1867–1960*. Princeton, N.J.: Princeton University Press, 1963.

Friend, Irwin, ed. *Study of the Savings and Loan Industry*, vols. I–IV. Washington, D.C.: Government Printing Office, July 1969.

Furlong, Frederick, and Michael Keeley. "Capital Regulation and Bank Risk-taking." *Journal of Banking and Finance* 13(December 1989):883–91.

Garcia, Gillian G. "FSLIC Is 'Broke' in More Ways than One." *The Financial Services Revolution: Policy Directions for the Future*. Edited by Catherine England and Thomas Huertas. Norwell, Mass.: Kluwer Academic Publishers, 1988.

Garcia, Gillian G., and Elizabeth Plautz. *The Federal Reserve: Lender of Last Resort*. Cambridge, Mass.: Ballinger Publishing Company, 1988.

Garcia, Gillian G., and Michael Polakoff. "Does Capital Forbearance Pay and If So, for Whom?" *Bank Structure and Competition*. Federal Reserve Bank of Chicago: 1985.

Garcia, Gillian G., et al. "The Garn-St Germain Depository Institutions Act of 1982." *Economic Perspectives*, Federal Reserve Bank of Chicago, April 1983.

Garrison, Roger W., Eugene D. Short, and Gerald P. O'Driscoll, Jr. "Financial Stability and FDIC Insurance." Research Working Paper No. 8410, October 1984.

Glassner, Daniel. "Abolish Deposit Insurance." *Wall Street Journal*, May 5, 1989.

Goldman, Laurie S., and Sherrill Shaffer. "The Economics of Deposit Insurance: A Critical Evaluation of Proposed Reform." *Yale Journal on Regulation* 2(1984):145–62.

Golembe, Carter H. "Development of Bank-Obligation Insurance and Some Comments on Its Economic Implications." Federal Deposit Insurance Corporation, 1958.

———. "The Deposit Insurance Legislation of 1933: An Examination of Its Antecedents and Its Purposes." *Political Science Quarterly* 25(June 1960):181–200.

Golembe, Carter H., and Stanley C. Silverberg. "Deposit Insurance Reform: A Framework for Analysis." Paper prepared by the Secura Group for the Association of Reserve City Bankers, September 1989.

Gorton, Gary. "Public Policy and the Evolution of Banking Markets." *Banking System Risk: Charting a New Course*. Federal Reserve Bank of Chicago: 1989.

———. "Clearing Houses and the Origin of Central Banking in the U.S." *Journal of Economic History* 45(1985):277–83.

159

Gorton, Gary, and Donald J. Mullineaux. "Joint Production of Confidence: Endogenous Regulation and the Nineteenth Century Commercial Bank Clearinghouses." *Journal of Money, Credit, and Banking* 19(November 1987):457–68.

Gray, Edwin J. Statement before the Senate Committee on Banking, Housing, and Urban Affairs. 100th Congress, 1st session. January 21, 1987.

Grundfest, Joseph A. "Lobbying into Limbo: The Political Ecology of the Savings and Loan Crisis." *Stanford Law and Policy Review* 2(Spring 1990):25–36.

Gup, Benton E. *Bank Fraud: Exposing the Hidden Threat to Financial Institutions.* Rolling Meadows, Ill.: Bank Administration Institute, 1990.

Guttenberg, Jack M., and Richard J. Herring. "Restructuring Depository Institutions." Wharton School, University of Pennsylvania. 1988. Mimeo.

Hammond, Bray. *Banks and Politics in America from the Revolution to the Civil War.* Princeton, N.J.: Princeton University Press, 1987.

Haraf, William S. "Financial Structure, the Safety-Net, and the Fallacy of 'Too Big to Fail.'" Paper prepared for conference, International Competitiveness in Financial Services. American Enterprise Institute, 1990.

Hempel, George H., Donald G. Simonson, Marvin L. Carlson, Marsha Simonson, and Marcia M. Cornett. "Market Value Accounting for Financial Service Companies." National Center for Financial Service Companies, University of California, Berkeley. 1989. Mimeo.

Hemphill, Robert H. Statement before the House Committee on Banking and Currency. 74th Congress, 1st session. 1935.

Hendershott, Patric H., and James D. Shilling. "The Continued Interest Rate Vulnerability of Thrifts." Undated mimeo.

Hess, Alan C. "Are Thrifts Worth Saving." Prepared for the Carnegie-Rochester Conference, April 1986. Mimeo.

Hill, John W., and Robert W. Ingram. "Selection of GAAP or RAP in the Savings and Loan Industry." *Accounting Review* 64(October 1989):667–79.

Hirschhorn, Eric. "Depositor Risk Perceptions and the Insolvency of the FSLIC." Office of Thrift Supervision. December 1989. Mimeo.

Horvitz, Paul M. "Assessing the Management Consignment Program." *Bank Structure and Competition.* Federal Reserve Bank of Chicago: 1987.

———. "Capital Is the Best Deposit Insurance Protector." *Outlook of the Federal Home Loan Bank System*, July/August 1987.

BIBLIOGRAPHY

———. "Deposit Insurance after Deregulation: A Residual Role for Regulation." *Identification and Control of Risk in the Thrift Industry.* Federal Home Loan Bank of San Francisco: 1983.

———. "Implications of the Texas Experience for Financial Regulation." *Banking System Risk: Charting a New Course.* Federal Reserve Bank of Chicago: 1989.

———. "Market Discipline Is Best Provided by Subordinated Creditors." *American Banker,* July 15, 1983.

———. "Subordinated Debt Is Key to New Bank Capital Requirements." *American Banker,* December 31, 1984.

———. "The Case against Risk-related Deposit Insurance Premiums." *Housing Finance Review* 2(July 1983):253–63.

———. "The FSLIC Crisis and the Southwest Plan." *American Economic Review* 79(May 1989):146–50.

Horvitz, Paul M., and R. Richardson Pettit. "Financial Services in the European Community: Implications for U.S. Financial Markets and Institutions." Paper prepared for conference, The United States and Europe in the 1990s. American Enterprise Institute, March 5–8, 1990.

Hoskins, W. Lee. "Reforming the Banking and Thrift Industries: Assessing Regulation and Risk." Frank M. Engle Lecture in Economic Security, American College, Bryn Mawr, Pennsylvania, May 22, 1989.

———. "Rethinking the Regulatory Response to Risk-Taking in Banking." *Economic Commentary,* Federal Reserve Bank of Cleveland, June 1, 1989.

Huertas, Thomas F. "Redesigning Financial Regulation." *Challenge* 31(January/February 1988):37–43.

———. "The Regulation of Financial Institutions: A Historical Perspective on Current Issues." In *Financial Services: The Changing Institutions and Government Policy.* Edited by George J. Benston. Englewood Cliffs, N.J.: Prentice-Hall, Inc., 1983.

Jackson, Brooks. *Honest Graft: Big Money and the American Political Process.* New York: Alfred A. Knopf, 1988.

Jacobs, Donald P., and Almarin Phillips. "Overview of the Commission's Philosophy and Recommendations." *Policies for a More Competitive Financial System.* Federal Reserve Bank of Boston: 1972.

James, Christopher. "The Costs of Liquidating Failed Banks." Working Paper Series, Garn Institute of Finance, November 1988.

Jones, Homer. "An Appraisal of the Rules and Procedures of Bank Supervision, 1929–39."*Journal of Political Economy* 98(February–December 1940):183–98.

———. "Some Problems of Bank Supervision." *Journal of the American Statistical Association* 33(June 1938):334–40.

161

Kane, Edward J. "Appearance and Reality in Deposit Insurance: The Case for Reform." *Journal of Banking and Finance* 10(June 1986):175–88.

———. "Confronting Incentive Problems in U.S. Deposit Insurance: The Range of Alternative Solutions." In *Deregulating Financial Services, Public Policy in Flux.* Edited by George G. Kaufman and Roger C. Kormendi. Cambridge, Mass.: Ballinger Publishing Co., 1986.

———. "Dangers of Capital Forbearance: The Case of the FSLIC and Zombie S&Ls." *Contemporary Policy Issues* 5(1987):77–83.

———. "Defective Regulatory Incentives and the Bush Initiative." August 1989. Mimeo.

———. "Deregulation, Savings and Loan Diversifications and the Flow of Housing Finance." *Savings and Loan Asset Management under Deregulation.* Federal Home Loan Bank of San Francisco: 1980.

———. "Good Intentions and Unintended Evil: The Case against Selective Credit Allocation." *Journal of Money, Credit, and Banking* 9(February 1977):55–69.

———. "How Incentive-Incompatible Deposit-Insurance Funds Fail." Prochnow Report No. PR-014, Madison, Wisc.: Prochnow Educational Foundation, 1988.

———. "Metamorphosis in Financial Services Delivery and Production." *Strategic Planning for Economic and Technological Change in the Financial Services Industry.* Federal Home Loan Bank of San Francisco: 1982.

———. "No Room for Weak Links in the Chain of Deposit Insurance Reform." *Journal of Financial Services Research* 1(September 1987):77–111.

———. "Principal-Agent Problems in S&L Salvage." *Journal of Finance* 45(1990):755–64.

———. "Short-changing the Small Saver: Federal Discrimination against the Small Saver during the Vietnam War." *Journal of Money, Credit, and Banking* 2(November 1970):513–22.

———. "S&Ls and Interest-Rate Regulation: The FSLIC as an In-Place Bailout Program." *Housing Finance Review* 1(July 1982):219–43.

———. "The Bush Plan Is No Cure for the S&L Malady." *Challenge* 46(November/December 1989):39–43.

———. *The Gathering Crisis in Federal Deposit Insurance.* Cambridge, Mass.: MIT Press, 1985.

———. "The Incentive Incompatibility of Government-sponsored Deposit Insurance Funds." Annual Meetings of the Econometric Society. Atlanta, Georgia, December 1989.

162

―――. "The Political Foundations of the Thrift Debacle: The Incentive Incompatibility of Government-sponsored Deposit Insurance Funds." Paper prepared for conference, Reform of Deposit Insurance and the Regulation of Depository Institutions in the 1990s: Setting the Agenda. Center for Economic Policy Research, Stanford University, May 18–19, 1990.

―――. "The Role of Government in the Thrift Industry's Net Worth Crisis." In *Financial Services: The Changing Institutions and Government Policy.* Edited by George J. Benston. Englewood Cliffs, N.J.: Prentice-Hall, 1983.

―――. *The S&L Insurance Mess: How Did It Happen?* Washington, D.C.: Urban Institute Press, 1989.

Kane, Edward J., and Haluk Unal. "Market Assessment of Deposit-Institution Riskiness." *Journal of Financial Services Research* 1(1988):207–29.

―――. "Modeling Structural and Temporal Variation in the Market's Valuation of Banking Firms." *Journal of Finance* 45(March 1990):113–36.

Kareken, John H. "Deposit Insurance Reform or Deregulation Is the Cart Not the Horse." *Quarterly Review,* Federal Reserve Bank of Minneapolis, Spring 1983.

―――. "The First Step in Bank Deregulation: What about the FDIC?" *American Economic Review* 73(May 1983):198–203.

Kareken, John H., and Neil Wallace. "Deposit Insurance and Bank Regulation." *Journal of Business* 51(July 1978):413–38.

Kaufman, George G. "Lender of Last Resort, Too Large to Fail and Deposit Insurance Reform." Paper prepared for conference, Reform of Deposit Insurance and the Regulation of Depository Institutions in the 1990s: Setting the Agenda. Center for Economic Policy Research, Stanford University, May 18–19, 1990.

―――. Statement before the Senate Committee on Banking, Housing, and Urban Affairs. 101st Congress, 2d session. May 22, 1990.

―――, ed. *Research in Financial Services.* Greenwich, Conn.: JAI Press, Inc., 1989.

―――. "The Truth about Bank Runs." In *The Financial Services Revolution: Policy Directions for the Future.* Edited by Catherine England and Thomas Huertas. Norwell, Mass.: Kluwer Academic Publishers, 1988.

Kaufman, George G., and Roger C. Kormendi, eds. *Deregulating Financial Services, Public Policy in Flux.* Cambridge, Mass.: Ballinger Publishing Co., 1986.

163

Kaufman, George G., and Larry R. Mote. "Securities Activities of Commercial Banks: The Current Economic and Legal Environment." *Staff Memoranda*. Federal Reserve Bank of Chicago: 1989.

Keehn, Silas. "Banking on the Balance, Powers, and the Safety Net: A Proposal." Federal Reserve Bank of Chicago, 1989.

Keeley, Michael C. "Deposit Insurance, Risk, and Market Power in Banking." *Banking System Risk: Charting a New Course*. Federal Reserve Bank of Chicago: 1989.

———. "Reforming Deposit Insurance." *Weekly Letter*. Federal Reserve Bank of San Francisco, April 21, 1989.

Keeley, Michael C., and Frederick Furlong. "A Reexamination of Mean-Variance Analysis of Bank Capital Regulation." *Journal of Banking and Finance*, forthcoming.

Kendall, Leon T. *The Savings and Loan Business*. Englewood Cliffs, N.J.: Prentice-Hall, 1962.

King, Jim. "Top Thrift Regulator Takes Hard Line against Fraud." *Atlanta Journal and Constitution*, July 28, 1990.

Kormendi, Roger C., Victor L. Bernard, S. Craig Pirrong, and Edward A. Snyder. *Crisis Resolution in the Thrift Industry*. Report of the Mid America Institute Task Force on the Thrift Crisis, March 3, 1989.

Kuprianov, Anatoli, and David L. Mengle. "The Future of Deposit Insurance: An Analysis of the Alternatives." *Economic Review*, Federal Reserve Bank of Richmond, May/June 1989.

Lea, Michael. "On the Front Lines of FIRREA." Paper prepared for the annual meetings of the Western Economic Association. San Diego, California, June 1990.

Lindow, Wesley. "Bank Capital and Risk Assets." *National Banking Review*, September 1963, pp. 29–46.

Lintner, John. *Mutual Savings Banks in the Savings and Mortgage Markets*. Andover, Mass.: Andover Press, Ltd., 1948.

Litan, Robert E. Statement before the Senate Judiciary Committee. 101st Congress, 2d session. August 14, 1990.

———. *What Should Banks Do?* Washington, D.C.: Brookings Institution, 1987.

Mahoney, Patrick I., and Alice P. White. "The Thrift Industry in Transition." *Federal Reserve Bulletin*, March 1985.

Maisel, Sherman J. *Risk and Capital Adequacy in Commercial Banks*. Chicago, Ill.: University of Chicago Press, 1981.

Malburn, William P., *What Happened to Our Banks*. Indianapolis, Ind.: Bobbs-Merrill Company, 1934.

Marcus, Alan J. "Deregulation and Bank Financial Policy." *Journal of Banking and Finance* 8(December 1984):557–65.

Marvell, Thomas B. *The Federal Home Loan Bank Board.* New York: Praeger, 1969.

McCanan, David. "Failure of Bank Guaranty Plans." *Federal Regulation of Banking.* Compiled by James Goodwin Hodgson. New York: Reference Shelf, H. W. Wilson Company, 1932.

McCarthy, Ian. "Deposit Insurance: Theory and Practice." *Staff Papers*, International Monetary Fund, September 1980.

Merton, Robert C. "An Analytic Derivation of the Cost of Deposit Insurance and Loan Guarantees." *Journal of Banking and Finance* 1(June 1977):3–11.

———. "On the Cost of Deposit Insurance When There Are Surveillance Costs." *Journal of Business*, 51(July 1978):439–52.

Murton, Arthur J. "Bank Intermediation, Bank Runs, and Deposit Insurance." *FDIC Banking Review* 7 (Spring/Summer 1989).

National Association of Mutual Savings Banks. *Mutual Savings Banking: Basic Characteristics and Role in the National Economy.* Englewood Cliffs, N.J.: Prentice-Hall, 1983.

Natter, Raymond. "Deregulation of Federal Savings Associations 1961 through 1982." Undated mimeo.

———. "Legislative History of the Garn-St Germain Act." Undated mimeo.

Nejezchleb, Lynn A., and Frederick S. Carns. "Deposit Insurance Oils the Financial System." *American Banker*, September 1, 1989.

Nelson, Richard W. "Management versus Economic Conditions as Contributors to the Recent Increase in Bank Failures." In *Financial Risk: Theory, Evidence and Implications.* Edited by Courtenay C. Stone. Norwell, Mass.: Kluwer Academic Publishers, 1986.

O'Connor, J. F. T. *Banking Act of 1935.* Hearings before the House Committee on Banking and Commerce. 74th Congress, 1st session. 1935.

O'Hara, M., and D. Easley. "The U.S. Postal Savings System in the Depression." *Journal of Economic History* 39(September 1979):741–53.

Osterberg, William P., and James B. Thomson. "Bank Capital Requirements and the Riskiness of Banks. A Review." *Economic Review*, Federal Reserve Bank of Cleveland, 1989.

Peltzman, Sam. "Entry in Commercial Banking." *Journal of Law & Economics* 8(October 1965):11–50.

165

Phelan, Richard J. *Record of the Special Outside Counsel in the Matter of Speaker James C. Wright, Jr.* House Committee on Standards of Official Conduct. Washington, D.C.: Government Printing Office, February 21, 1989.

Phillips, Almarin, and Donald P. Jacobs. "Reflections on the Hunt Commission." In *Financial Services: The Changing Institutions and Government Policy.* Edited by George J. Benston. Englewood Cliffs, N.J.: Prentice-Hall, 1983.

Pratt, Richard T. "Annual Report 1982." *Federal Home Loan Bank Board Journal* 15(April 1983):4–5.

———. Statement before the Senate Committee on Banking, Housing, and Urban Affairs. 100th Congress, 2d session. August 3, 1988.

Pyle, David H. "Comment on Bank Regulation and Monetary Policy." *Journal of Money, Credit, and Banking* 17(November 1985):722–24.

———. "The Losses on Savings Deposits from Interest Rate Regulations." *Bell Journal of Economics* 5(Autumn 1974):614–22.

Randall, Richard E. "Can the Market Evaluate Asset Quality Exposure in Banks?" *New England Economic Review*, Federal Reserve Bank of Boston, July/August 1989.

Report of the Task Force on Savings and Loan Portfolio Profitability. Prepared for the Board of Directors of the Federal Home Loan Bank of Little Rock and the Federal Home Loan Bank Board, July 1981.

Report on Combating Fraud, Abuse, and Misconduct in the Nation's Financial Institutions: Current Federal Efforts Are Inadequate. House Committee on Government Operations, October 13, 1988.

Riegle, Donald W., Jr. Statement on the Floor of the Senate. 101st Congress, 2d session. June 11, 1990.

Rolnick, Arthur J., and Warren E. Weber. "Inherent Instability in Banking: The Free Banking Experience." *Cato Journal* 5(Winter 1986):877–90.

———. "New Evidence on the Free Banking Era." *American Economic Review* 73(December 1983):1080–91.

Romer, Thomas, and Barry R. Weingast. "Congress; The Genesis of the Thrift Crisis. *Stanford Law and Policy Review* 2(Spring 1990):37–46.

———. "Political Foundations of the Thrift Debacle." Paper prepared for conference, Reform of Deposit Insurance and the Regulation of Depository Institutions in the 1990s: Setting the Agenda. Center for Economic Policy Research, Stanford University, Washington, D.C., May 18–19, 1990.

Ronn, Ehud I., and Avinash K. Verma. "Pricing Risk Adjusted Deposit Insurance: An Option-based Model." *Journal of Finance* 41(September 1986):871–96.

Rubinovitz, Robert. "How Does Financial Performance Influence a Thrift's Decision to Diversify?" Discussion paper, U.S. Department of Justice. May 30, 1989.

Ryon, Sandra L. "History of Bank Capital Adequacy Analysis." Working Paper No. 69-4, Division of Research, 1969.

Saunders, Anthony, Elizabeth Strock, and Nicholas G. Travlos. "Ownership Structure, Deregulation, and Bank Risk Taking." *Journal of Finance* 45(June 1990):643–54.

Schumer, Charles E., and J. Brian Graham. "The Unfinished Business of FIRREA." *Stanford Law and Policy Review* 2(Spring 1990):68–81.

Scott, Kenneth E. "Deposit Insurance and Bank Regulation: The Policy Choices." *Business Lawyer*, 44(May 1989):907–33.

———. "Never Again: The S&L Bailout Bill." Paper prepared for the twenty-sixth annual conference, Bank Structure and Competition. Federal Reserve Bank of Chicago, May 9–11, 1990.

Scott, Kenneth E., and Thomas Mayer. "Risk and Regulation in Banking: Some Proposals for Deposit Insurance." *Stanford Law Review* 23(May 1971):537–82.

Shadow Financial Regulatory Committee, Statement on an Outline of a Program for Deposit Insurance and Regulatory Reform, February 13, 1989.

Short, Eugenie D., and Jeffrey W. Gunther. *The Texas Thrift Situation: Implications for the Texas Financial Industry*. Occasional Paper, Financial Industry Studies Department, Federal Reserve Bank of Dallas, September 1988.

Short, Eugenie D., and Gerald P. O'Driscoll, Jr. "Deregulation and Deposit Insurance." *Economic Review*, Federal Reserve Bank of Dallas, September 1983.

Simonson, Donald G. and George H. Hempel. "Running on Empty: Accounting Strategies to Clarify Capital Values." *Stanford Law and Policy Review* 2(Spring 1990):92–101.

———. "Historical Perspective in Accounting for Financial Institutions' Performance." *Banking System Risk: Charting a New Course*. Federal Reserve Bank of Chicago: 1989.

Smith, Fred L., and Melanie S. Tammen. "Plugging America's Financial Black Holes: Reforming the Federal Deposit Insurance System." *Quarterly Report of Consumer Finance Law* 43(Winter 1989):44–48.

Sorkin, Alan L. *The Economics of the Postal System*. Lexington, Mass.: D.C. Heath and Company, 1980.

Spellman, Lewis J. *The Depository Firm and Industry: Theory, History, and Regulation*. New York: Academic Press, 1982.

Sprague, Irvine H. *Bailout: An Insider's Account of Bank Failures and Rescues*. New York: Basic Books, 1986.

————. "Deposit Insurance Is Crucial, despite What Pundits Say." *American Banker*, January 30, 1990.

Strunk, Norman, and Fred Case. *Where Deregulation Went Wrong: A Look at the Causes behind Savings and Loan Failures in the 1980s*. Chicago: U.S. League of Savings Institutions, 1988.

Summerfield, Arthur E. *The Story of the United States Postal Service*. New York: Holt, Rinehart and Winston, 1960.

Taggart, J. H., and L. D. Jennings. "The Insurance of Bank Deposits." *Journal of Political Economy* 42(February–December 1934):508–16.

Talley, S., and I. Mas. "Deposit Insurance in Developing Countries." Unpublished manuscript, World Bank, December 1989.

Tallman, Ellis. "Some Unanswered Questions about Bank Panics." *Economic Review*, Federal Reserve Bank of Atlanta, November/December 1988.

Tammen, Melanie S. "The Savings & Loan Crisis: Which Train Derailed—Deregulation or Deposit Insurance?" *Journal of Law & Politics* (Winter 1990).

Thomson, James B. "Economic Principles and Deposit-Insurance Reform." *Economic Commentary*, Federal Reserve Bank of Cleveland, May 15, 1989.

————. "The Use of Market Information in Pricing Deposit Insurance." *Journal of Money, Credit, and Banking* 19(November 1987):528–37.

————. "Using Market Incentives to Reform Bank Regulation and Federal Deposit Insurance." *Economic Review*, Federal Reserve Bank of Cleveland, 1990.

Thomson, James B., and Walker F. Todd. "Rethinking and Living with the Limits of Bank Regulation." *Cato Journal* 9(Winter 1990):579–600.

Tobin, James. "Deposit Insurance Must Go." *Wall Street Journal*, November 22, 1989.

Todd, Walker F. "A Brief History of International Lending from a Regional Banker's Perspective." *George Mason University Law Review* 11(Summer 1989):1–73.

————. "Developing Country Lending and Current Banking Conditions." *Economic Review*, Federal Reserve Bank of Cleveland, 1988.

168

BIBLIOGRAPHY

――――. "Lessons of the Past and Prospects for the Future in Lender of Last Resort Theory." *Bank Structure and Competition*, Federal Reserve Bank of Chicago, May 1988.

――――. "No Conspiracy, but a Convenient Forgetting: Dr. Pangloss Visits the World of Deposit Insurance." Cato Conference Paper, November 2, 1988.

U.S. Congress. House. Committee on Banking, Finance, and Urban Affairs. *Hearing on Transactions to Resolve Failed Depository Institutions*. 101st Congress, 2d session.

――――. *Interim Report from the Chairman of the RTC Task Force Subcommittee on Financial Institutions Supervision, Regulation and Insurance*. 101st Congress, 2d session. March 19, 1990.

U.S. Congress. House. Committee on Government Operations. *Combating Fraud, Abuse, and Misconduct in the Nation's Financial Institutions: Current Federal Efforts are Inadequate*. Seventy-second Report. Washington, D.C.: Government Printing Office, October 13, 1988.

U.S. General Accounting Office. Letter from Charles A. Bowsher, Comptroller General, to the Secretary of the Treasury on Deposit Insurance Reform. March 7, 1990.

Upham, Cyril B., and Edwin Lamke. *Closed and Distressed Banks*. Washington, D.C.: Brookings Institution, 1934.

Vartanian, Thomas P. "Regulatory Restructuring of Financial Institutions and the Rebirth of the Thrift Industry." *Legal Bulletin* 99(January 1983):1–22.

Wall, Larry D. "A Plan for Reducing Future Deposit Insurance Losses: Puttable Subordinated Debt." *Economic Review*, Federal Reserve Bank of Atlanta, July/August 1989.

Wall, M. Danny. Statement before the Senate Committee on Banking, Housing, and Urban Affairs. 101st Congress, 2d session. March 1, 1989.

Wallison, Peter J. *Back from the Brink: A Practical Plan for Privatizing Deposit Insurance and Strengthening Our Banks and Thrifts*. Washington, D.C.: American Enterprise Institute, 1990.

Walter, Ingo, ed. *Deregulating Wall Street: Commercial Bank Penetration of the Corporate Securities Market*. New York: John Wiley & Sons, 1985.

White, Eugene N. "Commercial Banks and Securities Markets: Lessons of the 1920s and 1930s for the 1980s and 1990s." *Banking System Risk: Charting a New Course*. Federal Reserve Bank of Chicago: 1989.

――――. *The Regulation and Reform of the American Banking System, 1900–1929*. Princeton, N.J.: Princeton University Press, 1983.

169

White, Lawrence J. "Mark to Market Accounting Is Vital to FSLIC and Valuable to Thrifts." *Outlook of the Federal Home Loan Bank System,* January/February 1988.

———. "Mark-to-Market: A (Not So) Modest Proposal." *Financial Managers' Statement,* January/February 1990.

———. "Market Value Accounting: An Important Part of the Reform of the Deposit Insurance Systems." *Capital Issues in Banking.* Washington, D.C.: Association of Reserve City Bankers, 1988.

———. "The Case for Mark-to-Market Accounting." *Secondary Mortgage Markets* 7(Summer 1990):2–4.

———. "Problems of the FSLIC: A Former Policy Maker's View." *Contemporary Policy Issues* 8(April 1990):62–81.

———. "The Reform of Federal Deposit Insurance." *Journal of Economic Perspectives* 3(Fall 1989):11–29.

———. "The Value of Market Value Accounting for the Deposit Insurance System." *Journal of Accounting, Auditing, and Finance,* forthcoming.

White, Lawrence J., and Edward L. Golding. "Collateralized Borrowing at Thrifts Poses Risk to FSLIC." *American Banker,* February 24, 1989.

Williamson, Stephen D. "Bank Failures, Financial Restrictions, and Aggregate Fluctuations: Canada and the United States, 1870–1913." *Quarterly Review,* Federal Reserve Bank of Minneapolis, Summer 1989.

Willis, H. Parker, and John M. Chapman. *The Banking Situation.* New York: Columbia University Press, 1934.

Woerheide, Walter J. *The Savings and Loan Industry: Current Problems and Possible Solutions.* Westport, Conn.: Quorom Books, 1984.

Woodward, G. Thomas. "Deposit Guarantees in Other Countries." *Congressional Research Report for Congress.* Congressional Research Service, Library of Congress, November 1989.

———. "FSLIC, the Budget, and the Economy." Congressional Research Service, Library of Congress. January 12, 1989. Mimeo.

———. "The Economics of Deposit Insurance." *Congressional Research Report for Congress.* Congressional Research Service, Library of Congress, November 1989.

The Working Group of the Cabinet Council on Economic Affairs. *Recommendations for Change in the Federal Deposit Insurance System.* January 1985.